FEB 4 2005

TWO BEETHOVEN SKETCHBOOKS

TWO BEETHOVEN SKETCHBOOKS

A description with musical extracts

by

GUSTAV NOTTEBOHM

Translated by
JONATHAN KATZ

With a Foreword by
DENIS MATTHEWS

LONDON
VICTOR GOLLANCZ LTD
1979

ISBN 0 575 02583 2

Photoset and printed in Great Britain by
Lowe & Brydone Printers Limited, Thetford, Norfolk

CONTENTS

Translator's note vii
Foreword by Denis Matthews ix

A SKETCHBOOK OF 1802
 Introduction 3
 The Sketchbook 9
 Notes 39

A SKETCHBOOK OF 1803
 Introduction 47
 The Sketchbook 50
 Notes 120

Index of Names 127
Index of Compositions 129

TRANSLATOR'S NOTE

As THIS BOOK is intended as no more than an English translation of Nottebohm's two monographs, without any original contribution to Beethoven scholarship, editorial comments (footnotes marked 'Transl.') have been kept to a minimum. I have considered it helpful to give the appropriate references to standard and available English editions of secondary works cited by Nottebohm, but at the same time left the original references in the main body of the text. Brief bibliographical details of the English works are given below. The choice of musical terminology inevitably raises problems, and I have attempted here to use acceptable English technical terms without departing too far from those used by Nottebohm. Thus, for example, the sections of a standard sonata-form movement are given as 'exposition', 'development' etc. (for German *ester Teil, zweiter Teil*), while, following Tovey and others, I have generally eschewed the term 'second subject' and substituted such terms as 'first part of the second group', for German *erster Seitensatz*, and 'end-section' (instead of the strangely prevalent 'codetta') for *Schlußsatz* or *Schlußpartie*. At all events, Nottebohm's own references to bar numbers etc. should preclude ambiguity.

In 1924 Paul Mies brought out a second edition of the monographs and appended an index of compositions cited. A similar list is added at the end of this translation.

I am happy to acknowledge with gratitude the help and advice offered by Mr Balint Vazsonyi, by my father, by Mr Peter Ward Jones and Mr Rembert Herbert, and above all my thanks are due to Denis Matthews, who read the typescript and made many valuable suggestions.

J. K.

English editions cited in the notes:
Thayer's Life of Beethoven (revised and edited by Elliot Forbes), 2 vols., Princeton 1964.

The Letters of Beethoven, coll., transl., and edited with an introduction, appendixes, notes and indexes by Emily Anderson, 3
vols., London 1961.

Beethoven as I knew him, A Biography by Anton Felix Schindler,
ed. by D. W. MacArdle, transl. by Constance S. Jolly, London
1966.

For background reading on Beethoven's sketches etc. readers
may be referred to the two chapters by Alan Tyson in *The
Beethoven Companion,* ed. by Denis Arnold and Nigel Fortune,
London 1971.

FOREWORD

MOST SERIOUS DISCUSSIONS of Beethoven's music refer back
sooner or later to Gustav Nottebohm's researches into the
sketchbooks. In fact his name is so often cited by others that it is
surprising to find no English translation of his works readily
available. Admittedly the art of musicology has refined itself in
the intervening century into something approaching an exact
science. Research has gained in precision from an accumulation
of knowledge and skills, aided by modern methods of detection
and communication. Nowadays hardly a watermark passes un-
examined. Even an ink-blot may help in dating or identifying a
random page of manuscript. Such fastidiousness is fully justified
in the endless quest for the truth in historical matters. It is more
than justified where those matters concern the creation of great
works of art. Though it is sometimes held that musical theorists
tend to get lost in a world of their own, their direct or indirect
effect on live music-making is vital. Today we have on the whole
better and more authentic editions of the classics. We live in an
Urtext age and rightly so. The desire to know exactly what a
composer wrote sums up our respect for the past and our re-
sponsibility towards it.

The Beethoven sketchbooks come into a rather different
category. They contain, for the most part, musical ideas in
embryo and were never intended, let alone prepared, for the
perusal of others. Their general history is fairly well known.
Having been kept with care by Beethoven himself they were sold
off at the auction after his death and widely scattered. Only a few
of the books survived intact, but many more were mutilated or
lost over the years. Yet their value and fascination—not only for
the genuine researcher but for the performer and the enquiring
music-lover—were gradually realized. The chance of studying
such great music in the making and in such detail was unique.
Other composers obviously made sketches but no comparable
master to our knowledge recorded the workings of his mind so

systematically and laboriously. And so the researchers set to work, tracking down the surviving material, deciphering Beethoven's rough notes and identifying them where possible. The process still continues with all its attendant problems, though the prospect of a complete analysis of the known sketches and sketchbooks seems remote indeed.

Nottebohm was by far the most famous pioneer in this field. He was born at Lüdenscheid in Westphalia in 1817. In 1846 he settled in Vienna where he became known as a pianist, teacher, editor and composer. His research interests produced an important thematic catalogue of Beethoven's works and a whole series of essays and commentaries on the sketchbooks. These have come down to us under four main headings, two of them analyses of specific sketchbooks and two of them collections of various papers and articles, *Beethoveniana* and *Zweite Beethoveniana*. The last of these was published posthumously in 1887 and edited by Mandyczewski: it runs to nearly six hundred pages and affords a random but remarkably wide survey of sketches from all periods of Beethoven's mature creative life. Nottebohm had died in 1882, and the last twenty years of his life had been largely absorbed with his Beethoven studies, despite his attention to Schubert and Mozart. The two commentaries on individual sketchbooks concern us here. The first, dealing with the so-called 'Kessler' sketchbook of 1802 and thereabouts, was published by Breitkopf und Härtel in 1865; the second, which examined 'Landsberg 6' and produced the important sketches for the *Eroica*, appeared in 1880. These two studies were later bound together and issued under the title *Zwei Skizzenbücher* and in this form they now reappear in English.

Titles like 'Kessler', 'Landsberg 6', 'Wielhorsky' and so forth have been adopted by scholars to identify sketchbooks from the names of their former owners. Thus a collection of Beethoven manuscripts in the British Museum, many of them sketches, is referred to as the 'Kafka' miscellany. This was published in 1970, the bicentenary of Beethoven's birth, and splendidly edited by Joseph Kerman, who offered the entire contents in facsimile and ordinary music-type, skilfully separating out the recognisable from the unidentifiable fragments. Nottebohm, as a single-handed enthusiast working over a century ago, had neither the means nor the immediate desire for such comprehensiveness.

He was inevitably selective and to some extent subjective. Yet Kerman, in his preface to the 'Kafka' publication, praised Nottebohm as 'the still recognised master' despite reservations about his methods. 'He made some mistakes,' wrote Kerman, 'but it is to be doubted whether many musical scholars have maintained so high a standard of accuracy and objectivity, and so sharp a sense of the relevant, in treating a similar mass of difficult material.'

Many modern scholars have paid similar tributes to Notte-bohm and all are indebted to him for the stimulus he gave to the whole subject of the sketchbooks. His commentaries have become 'classic' and as such have been reprinted from time to time in the original German. Their circulation has never been vast, though many of the music examples have been copiously quoted by others, especially those concerning the genesis of familiar themes and masterstrokes. It is easy enough to jump to conclusions, to simplify the evidence, and to arouse incredulity at the vast gap between an early sketch and the finished product. For this reason perhaps there has been some reluctance on the part of experts to admit a more 'popular' approach. Yet a close-up view of Beethoven at work may deepen the general music-lover's appreciation of him and provide valuable insights for the per-former. No conductor of the *Eroica* should fail to study the extensive sketches for it. No pianist or string-player can afford to miss the new light thrown by the sketchbooks on the sonatas and quartets, including the cross-influences between different media.

It was Nottebohm who first placed most of this material at our disposal. Many others have since examined specific aspects and details of the sketches with still greater thoroughness and forensic zeal. It would be an endless task to attempt to up-date or correct Nottebohm. Since his researches and commentaries have earned their own place in musical history it would even seem presumptuous to do so. In this spirit, and with the minimum of editorial remarks, they are offered hopefully to a wider public of Beethoven admirers.

25 MAY 1978   DENIS MATTHEWS

A SKETCHBOOK OF 1802

INTRODUCTION

SINGLE SKETCHES AND brief reports on Beethoven's notebooks have often been published, but a full, page-by-page description of an entire sketchbook with musical extracts, enabling the reader to gain an impression of its character and contents, has not yet been undertaken. The present work is an attempt at such a project.

Our subject is an oblong-folio (teatro) notebook of 192 pages, with sixteen staves on each page. Apart from a few places left blank, it is filled with sketches or drafts in Beethoven's hand for various kinds of composition. Unlike many others, this notebook is not made up of separate sheets strung together, but is properly bound by a bookbinder; it is trimmed and has a firm pasteboard cover. It was bound in this form before it was used for writing. This seemingly trivial detail becomes especially significant because the sketchbook is now preserved in entirety not only as it left the bookbinder but also as Beethoven laid it aside; it is complete with all its pages and there is nowhere any sign of a page having been partially or completely torn out. Such completeness is seldom found, and it allows us, as far as is possible with sketchbooks, to make an uninterrupted observation of Beethoven's working method; in our consideration of the sketches it dispels any fear of an omission resulting from such defects.

The sketchbook was bought at the auction of Beethoven's estate by the late piano-maker Carl Stein and is now in the possession of the well-known composer and pianist, Mr J. C. Kessler, in Vienna.

No external evidence is available for determining the time at which the sketchbook was written. Nevertheless, some indication is to be obtained from research in other quarters. The earliest date that can be considered certain, by determining the time at which the compositions worked on in the book were completed or published, is during April 1802. Moreover the

3

compositions to which the last pages of the book refer were ready for press towards the end of that year. But although the outer limits of the period in question are thus certain, it should still be remembered that some time would have passed between the draft and its completion or publication; a slightly earlier date must therefore be assumed. Other factors must also be considered. In the summer and autumn of 1802 Beethoven was living in the country. It is likely that while he was there he made use of writing materials for taking notes, and that the materials he chose were suitable for use during outdoor walks. Our sketchbook, however, is written throughout in ink, and there is no sign of any pencil markings. It can be assumed therefore that it was used at his desk at home, probably during the winter months. Besides, a stiff-covered book of this size would hardly have been convenient for outdoor use in the country. Another consideration is that in the first quarter of the sketchbook there are groups of various dances of a kind which was particularly popular in Vienna at the turn of the century. We can only explain their presence by assuming that they were written for some occasion and by connecting them with the kind of dances that are held in the winter. Taking these and other observations into account, we can with a fair degree of certainty assume that the sketchbook was used roughly between October 1801 and May 1802. It may be conjectured that Beethoven used the book while he was housebound because of an illness which occurred during this period (cf. Wegeler, *Biographische Notizen*, pp. 38 ff., and p. 98; also Schindler's *Biographie*, pp. 85 ff. in the 3rd edition), though our knowledge concerning this illness is not sufficiently exact for certainty.

The sketches are written mostly in one part—i.e. on a single stave and rarely on two or more. It is to be assumed *a priori* that they were written more or less in the form and order in which they appear on the pages of the book. A fleeting look through the whole book does not seem to contradict this assumption. Nevertheless on closer scrutiny we must qualify it a little. It can be seen that Beethoven's normal habit was to start a new piece on a fresh page, and also that he very frequently worked on different movements alternately or simultaneously. As a result different groups of sketches were often crammed so closely together that, in order to find more space, he sooner or later had to use and fill

4

pages previously left blank, and eventually the sketches for very different pieces necessarily came together pell-mell and ran on side by side. In the resulting medley it is difficult to retain the main thread and not to lose the direction and continuity. Nevertheless, the reliability of information offered by the original completeness of the book suggests that we may set some value on the examination of such evidence, and it will be seen that the conclusions in this respect of the following study are based on an exact comparison and detailing of the individual groups of sketches. In those places where it is not possible to establish with certainty the pattern and succession of sketches, it will be preferable to say little or nothing about them.

We cannot now enter in detail into Beethoven's procedure in writing sketches, nor into his general working method. Such a study will only be possible when at least the evidence of a fairly significant number of sketchbooks is available. The present treatise must be restricted to the most important evidence of this one sketchbook and to some general observations. We must remember here again Beethoven's habit of working at more than one piece simultaneously, and the fact that as a rule he started a new piece before completing one begun earlier. This can be seen throughout almost the entire sketchbook. In fact Beethoven elsewhere talked about it himself; in a letter (cf. Wegeler, *Biographische Notizen*, p. 27) of June 29th 1800*—i.e. somewhat earlier than the sketchbook—he wrote to Wegeler: 'I live only in my music; hardly is one piece started when I have begun another. As I am writing now, I often work at three or four compositions at the same time.' However, in spite of this unsystematic procedure it is evident that as a rule Beethoven was clear about his objectives from the start; he remained true to his original conceptions, and once an idea was grasped, he carried it through to the end. But sometimes the opposite is the case, and some places are to be found where in the course of composing Beethoven was diverted from his first idea, with the result that the end product appeared quite different from the original sketch. Apart from such cases, which can only be observed in completed works, the book has also a fair number of unfinished

*For a full translation of this letter, *vid.* Emily Anderson's edition, Vol. I p. 57. (The suggested date there is 1801) [Transl.]

sketches, and in these the work generally did not progress beyond the very first draft.

So much for our observations when we consider the sketches in their broadest outlines. It is however far more fascinating to look at them in detail and see how Beethoven operated in individual cases—how he began a piece, advanced step by step, stopped short, modified, combined, developed etc.—and how he proceeded in various stages from the initial conception to the final product, and how all these steps are revealed by the extracts shown below.

In general it can be seen that in all the work undertaken in his sketchbooks Beethoven approached the task in many different ways, sometimes achieving his aim by opposite methods. We notice this variety especially if we compare sketches for movements different in themselves but belonging to the same genre of composition. It is possible to distinguish two entirely different methods. Both are attested in corresponding groups of sketches. In one kind the thematic formation is pre-eminent; the first sketch ends abruptly with the main theme and the ensuing work is restricted to modifying and developing the already established basic core until it appears suitable for realization. Then the same course is followed with the subsidiary subjects, and always it is separate beginnings that are found, rather than an entirety. We encounter the entirety only outside the sketchbook in the final, printed work, where the sections that lie scattered in the sketchbook are united. In the other type of sketch this kind of thematic mosaic work is excluded; each sketch is aimed at an entirety and presents a complete picture. The very first sketch gives the full outline of a section of a movement; then the sketches that follow appear as complete revisions of the first, as different readings, in which the object is sometimes to modify the general character, sometimes to reshape in broad outline, to develop the subsidiary subjects etc. These two types of method could hardly be more different. Of course the majority of the sketches belong to neither type exclusively, but rather fluctuate between the two. Such variety makes it impossible to discover in the work one definite order and one single procedure common to all cases. Beethoven, then, did not move in a rut;* he was free from any such conventional pro-

*This is so obvious that it may seem superfluous to elaborate. We must

6

cedure. Once this is shown, it is clear that the sketchbooks will not reveal the inner law which guided Beethoven's creative work. Investigation of this would necessarily involve abandoning the standpoint of a superficial consideration of the sketches and at least attempting to work on another, more profound level.

It is possible for us to observe the gradual development of a plant and acquaint ourselves with the stages of its growth. Following certain fixed laws it undergoes continuous change and constantly manifests something new; but all that is new is still the old, and a genetic explanation is possible. Musical creation is a different process; generally it is bound to the expression of something particular and individual, and in this individuality it does not follow a law of nature, as does the plant; the laws it follows are spiritual. We can consider a piece of music both as a whole and in its details. We can analyse its structure and rejoice in its beauty. But its genesis, and how it came to be as it is, elude us. Because of the self-contained, completed form in which it appears, there remain no traces indicative of a preceding process of development. If we understand it as an organic formation, we must assume that it arose organically and that it developed outwards into a unified whole. It is of course true that the sketchbooks, in which the firm, immutable material of the final composition appears, as it were, in flux, disclose something of the process of origin, discovery, formation etc. But we must understand quite clearly that there is much they do not reveal, and that we learn least of all from them about what we call 'organic'. What is missing in them, we can gather only by speculation. We may seek it in Beethoven the artist himself, in the unity of his whole character and spirit, and in the harmony of his inner powers. In order to visualize the unity of realization and idea, it is necessary to consider the whole person together with his intellectual and spiritual activities. Herein one may also find the key to his technical execution. But who can really boast that he has full knowledge of, or is in possession of, such keys?

---

remember, however, the numerous recent attempts at turning Beethoven's working method (under one name or another) into common property and a branch of study. Quite apart from this it seems desirable to be as clear as possible in our minds about the standpoint we should adopt in our study of a sketchbook.

In the selection of certain sketches for publication here, those have been chosen which appear noteworthy for artistic or other reasons. The majority are reproduced in full, as they appear in the book; those which are abbreviated are indicated as such. Thus where one of the longer sketches breaks off, or appears to break off, abruptly, this is the case in Beethoven's manuscript, as is also the sign 'etc.'. Passages which are illegible or of doubtful orthography are marked as such by a question mark in brackets (?). It is of the many uncompleted and unknown sketches that fewest are suitable for reproduction here; in the majority of cases a brief mention of them is sufficient. Most of the information properly belonging to a historical commentary etc. is to be found in the notes appended to the end of the text.

THE SKETCHBOOK

THE SKETCHBOOK BEGINS (pp. 1–5) with some dance-type pieces in ¾ time, apparently minuets. The words 'Corni', 'Bassi soli' etc., which appear in certain places, indicate that they were intended for orchestra. None of them has been published. We do not even know whether Beethoven worked out the drafts in completion. The intended orchestral setting and the genre itself make it likely that they were meant for a ball or some similar occasion.[1] We give here the drafts of two of the pieces:

There follow (pp. 6–13) several drafts for the 'Opferlied' by Matthisson, 'Die Flamme lodert'. We know of two settings by Beethoven of this text, one for solo voice with piano accompaniment, the other for solo voice with choir and orchestra (Op. 121).

The two settings have much in common. The drafts on these pages are for the first setting.[2] The first and one of the last are given here:

Immediately after this come (on pp. 14–28) drafts for a recitative and aria on the words 'No, non turbarti, o Nice' and 'Ma tu tremi, o mio tesoro' etc. The text is taken from a cantata by

Metastasio (*La Tempesta*). With regard to figuration etc., two
types of draft are distinguishable, one with rich coloratura and
extended notes:

ma tu tre-mi o mi-o te-so-ro ma tu pal-pi-ti cor mi-o

io par - - ti - ro

nice in-gra - - - - - - - ta io par-ti-ro

par - - - - - - ti - ro.

These characteristics point to the design of a concert or bravura
aria. The later and last drafts agree essentially with the earlier
ones, but the figuration is greatly simplified and only in part
retained. Beethoven later worked out the drafts of the last version in a setting for soprano, 2 violins, viola, bass and 'cello. The
piece remains unpublished.[3] The thematic opening of the aria in
the last version is as follows:

Ma tu tre-mi, o mio te-so-ro, ma tu pal-pi-ti, cor mi-o.

Amongst these sketches we find (on pp. 16–19), in addition to
other pieces, the start of a movement, no doubt intended for the
second symphony:

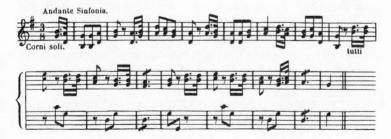

Andante Sinfonia.

Corni soli. tutti

There are also the drafts for three country dances. These are to be found among the twelve orchestral dances;[4] in the order in which they appear in the sketchbook they are nos. 10 (C major), 2 (A major) and 9 (A major) in that collection.[5] We can deduce from their order and context in the sketchbook that they were written out before the conclusion of the sketches for the aria 'Ma tu tremi'.

Immediately after the sketches for the Italian aria comes (p. 28) a draft for the 6th Bagatelle of Op. 33:

The position of the piece in the book shows that it must have been written after the sketches for the aria were finished, and also after the three dances. Comparison of this sketch with the printed version reveals that the latter represents a later reading.[6]

On pp. 29–32 there follow various sketches, mostly for unknown pieces and unfinished; from them we give one extract here:

The next eleven pages (33–43) bear uninterrupted sketches for the last movement of the Symphony in D major.[7] Apart from small fragments and drafts which are concerned with the subsidiary subjects, three longer or major drafts can be discerned. These, though partially incomplete, hang together and bear survey and comparison. The first draft has only a part of the principal subject we know in the printed version:

Also the two subsidiary subjects (or 'subsidiary' and 'final' subjects) are missing, and instead of them there is a different, unknown subsidiary subject.

The second draft contains the second subsidiary subject, but the first is lacking:

Both of these drafts break off at the end of the first part of the movement.

The third draft extends over the whole finale:

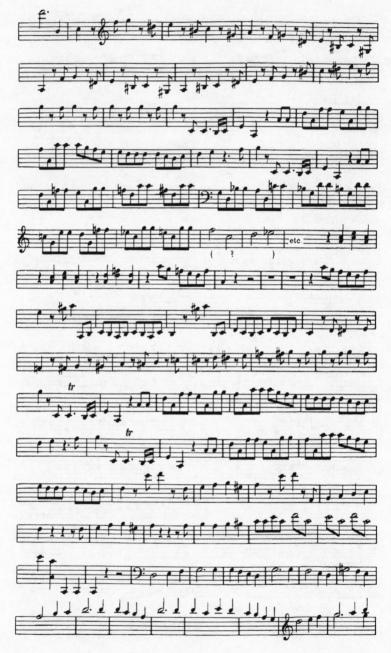

17

Remarkably here the second subsidiary subject is missing in the first part of the movement, but it does appear in the second and fourth parts, so that the form approaches that of a Rondo. From the remaining sketches we give here an isolated fragment:

After this movement for the D major symphony come more dances in ³⁄₄ time (pp. 44 and 45). Only a part of them has been published; they are nos. 1, 2, 3, 4 and 6 in the collection *Sechs ländlerische Tänze*.[8]

Some sketches for unknown pieces (pp. 46 and 47) are followed on pp. 48–73 by the terzet 'Tremate, empi, tremate', sketched here in full and published as Op. 116. Beethoven probably laid the draft aside for many years before working it out fully or making a fair copy.[9]

The sketches we have seen so far belong to a wide variety of musical genres, including dances, songs, and piano and orchestral movements. The sketches that follow are with few exceptions concerned with compositions for piano with or without some other instrument.

The first (p. 74) is the abruptly ended start of the first movement of the sonata for piano and violin in A major, Op. 30 no. 1, followed on the same line by another phrase, similarly terminated, which Beethoven probably intended to use in the same work:[10]

Further work on this movement extends over 22 pages (74–95) with long interruptions. The first interruption is by a canon; then there are some unknown fragments, drafts for the second movement of the same sonata, and finally some drafts for the third movement of the sonata Op. 47.

The following sample from the unknown fragments (p. 74) is a piece which was probably intended originally for the last movement of the A major sonata, Op. 30 no. 1:

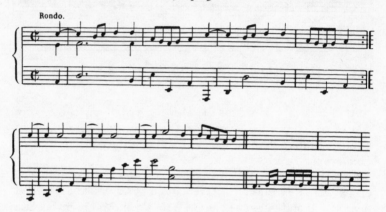

The canon (p. 75) runs as follows:

A few observations may help to explain this piece. At the turn of the century there was a great deal of hair-splitting discussion as to whether the new century began with the year 1800 or 1801. Even the musical world turned its hand to finding a solution. In the *Leipziger allgemeine musikalische Zeitung* of 18th September 1799 there appeared an article attempting to demonstrate with a canon that 1801 was the first year of the 19th century; but the author (Wr. in D.) then grows uncertain and eventually leaves the question undecided. A reply to the article came on 1st January 1800, written in 'Wien, den 21. December 1799'. The second article, signed simply 'Fr.', draws attention to the confusion between cardinal and ordinal numbers and seeks to settle the vexed question similarly with a 4-part canon. The canon is none other than the one in Beethoven's sketchbook. It is hard to say what prompted Beethoven to copy it out. He cannot have composed it; it appears in the sketchbook without any sign of correction, with no preliminary drafts, and only in the form of a 'finite canon', as printed in the newspaper. Certainly Beethoven made other similar copies of pieces elsewhere, but there is no original canon in the sketchbooks without the necessary drafts.[11]

In among the work on the first movement of the A major sonata Op. 30 no. 1 there are also, as already mentioned, the sketches for the second movement (pp. 87–97), of which the following is the first self-contained draft for the opening section:

On pp. 88–107 we find the sketches for the final movement of the Op. 47 sonata. Here again we give the first draft for the opening:

We notice here that Beethoven worked on the three movements simultaneously, and it is more than likely that they were originally intended to go together to form a sonata.[12]

Among the sketches for the last movement of the Op. 47 sonata we find also (p. 101) the first fragmentary sketches for the first and last movements of the sonata in C minor for piano and violin, Op. 30 no. 2. They are as follows:

22

We can tell from the position of these sketches that they were made before the end of the last movement of the Op. 47 sonata was written down. There is some noteworthy material also among the further sketches for the first movement of the C minor sonata (pp. 108–119). The second fragmentary opening runs thus (p. 108):

etc.

There are also the original and variant readings of the march-like subsidiary subject in E-flat major (p. 109):

Then on p. 110:

and on p. 113:

After the first drafts for the two outer movements of this sonata there emerge gradually those for the two middle movements. First comes the Adagio (pp. 108–128) with its fragmentary opening, appearing here in G major:

Then the Scherzo (pp. 120–129):

At last on pp. 122–139 the final movement is taken up again. Once more the placing of the sketches, in which the movements of the sonata appear intermingled, shows that Beethoven worked on several movements at once.

The work on the sonata is interrupted by the following pieces:

(p. 117) opening of the 5th Bagatelle in C minor from Op. 119 (Op. 112 in the older Vienna edition);[13]

(pp. 124 and 131) the theme for the final movement of the sonata in A major, Op. 30 no. 1;

(pp. 125 and 129) passages related to the second and third movements of the sonata in G major, Op. 30 no. 3;

(p. 130) a sketch for the first movement of the piano sonata in D minor, Op. 31 no. 2.

In addition there are various fragments for unknown pieces. All these were written down before the work on the C minor sonata was finished. From the unknown pieces the following extract is a composition for piano, with pedal and fingering marks added (p. 135):

26

We shall pass over the final movement of the A major sonata and consider it in context below.

Of great interest is the draft for the first movement of the D minor piano sonata, Op. 31 no. 2:[14]

27

Beethoven does not here embark on modifying and developing the various themes and motives as he does in many other sketches, but rather notes down in broad outline a whole structure; however he gives only the opening and conclusion, as it were the corner stones, and omits all the transitional and episodic sections. There is no trace of the other movements of this sonata, except perhaps for a hint of the motive of the last

28

movement in the beginning of the E-flat major piece shown above.[15]

The next notable group of sketches is concerned with the three movements of the G major sonata for piano and violin, Op. 30 no. 3. From the sketches for the first movement (pp. 140–146) the following is the first draft of the principal subject; it shows that the distinctive rolling character of the theme as we know it was not entirely spontaneous.

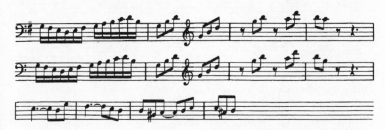

In another respect the first sketches for the second movement (pp. 125 and 143–149) are also remarkable. They show how the principal melody of the movement was in fact a combination of two different melodies. The first version is found in a phrase on p. 125 among some earlier sketches:

Later (pp. 143 and 145) there appears a melodic structure closely related to this, and indeed in bars 4–8 almost identical:

But on the same page there is another, quite different melody:

Immediately next to this (p. 143) is the first sketch which corresponds to the final version we know of the theme. It is formed by a combination of the melodies above; an answering phrase (bars 4–8) is taken from the first or second melody into the last:

This may indeed be called a 'composition' in the very strictest sense.[16] The other melodic sections of this second movement also had to undergo transformation before attaining their final form, for example the following fragment (p. 145), of which Beethoven eventually retained only the bass part:

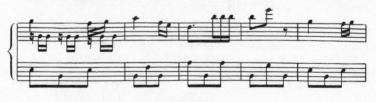

30

On page 147 we find the following:

and

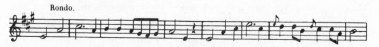

The movement is an excellent example of 'piecemeal' formation.

The sketches for the third movement (pp. 144–154) are from the outset fairly close to the final version. The position of the sketches for the G major sonata shows that Beethoven worked simultaneously on the first and second movements, as also on the second and third.

The final movement of the A major piano and violin sonata Op. 30 no. 1 deserves further comment. A fragment of it is found among the sketches for the C minor sonata (p. 124). Here is the upper part of the theme:

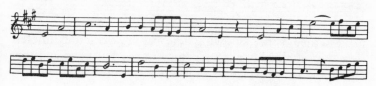

The 'Rondo' marking, and also a fragment after this in the same time and in the relative minor, apparently intended to form an episodic subject, leave no doubt that Beethoven originally had the Rondo form in mind. A few pages later (p. 131) the same theme reappears, but in a quite different form and more complete; however there is no marking as to the shape or form of the movement in which it was to come:

31

It appears again later (pp. 146 and 154–161) as a theme for variations, and together with them, between and after sketches for the G major sonata Op. 30 no. 3. This position shows not only that the movement was written later than the final movement of Op. 47, but also that it was written last of all the movements of the three sonatas of Op. 30.[17]

After several pages of unrecognizable sketches we find on pp. 164–179 a second set of variations, this time those for piano in E-flat major, Op. 35. First of all the 3rd, 5th and 11th variations are outlined thematically and partially worked out; later on come also the 8th, 1st, 2nd, 4th and 15th variations. The sketches for the introductory variations over the bass part of the theme (*a due, a tre, a quattro*) do not appear until later, in the course of further work and partly on four staves, as for string quartet. The theme, the *Finale alla fuga* etc. are lacking, but there are some sketches, with the title *Finale presto,* for a more extended movement in $^2/_4$ time which was never published. This employs a free treatment of the theme and has the standard character of a Finale. If we look at the whole group of sketches it seems that Beethoven first intended to write a conventional set of variations like those on *Vieni amore,* but while working on them he became aware of the possibilities of the ground bass and resourcefulness of the theme, and consequently was led to compose some variations in a more serious vein. Apparently he came back to the work and completed it elsewhere; nothing more is found in the sketchbook. The above sketches are thus to be considered as preliminary work.[18]

Amongst the group of sketches for the E-flat variations there appears also (p. 176) the principal motive for the theme of the piano variations in F major, Op. 34:

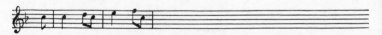

Next to them is the following note: 'Each variation in different time—or alternately passages once in the left hand and then almost the same passages or others in the right hand'. Somewhat later (p. 180) there is a four-bar fragment in ⁶⁄₈ time relating to the beginning of the final F major variation. In these fragments we see the beginning of some new work which Beethoven must have continued and completed elsewhere, since no more of it appears in the sketchbook. We see also that he conceived the idea of the F major variations before those in E-flat were finished.[19]

After various sketches and fragments of unknown pieces there are some drafts (pp. 182–190) for the first movement of the piano sonata in G major, Op. 31 no. 1. From the various other sketches we give here a fragment for string quartet (p. 175):

The anticipatory chords and staccato bass notes are surely the origin of the closely related principal motive in the sonata movement which follows soon after. The first sketch for this movement goes only as far as the end of the exposition and still differs quite considerably from the final version, compared with which it has a rather lighter, gayer character. However the close relation of the two is clear throughout:

A second draft (pp. 186–190) extends over the whole movement and comes very close to the final version, apart from the coda, in which the motive

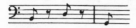

is more prominent:[20]

Between these sketches we find also parts of the other two movements of the sonata, as well as three different fragments, each entitled '*Sonata 2da*', for example this beautiful fragment:

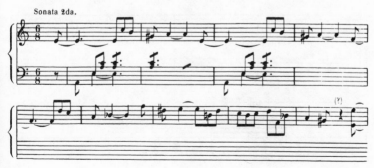

Of the Rondo of the G major sonata we find little more than the principal theme. The second movement is more complete, but only in scattered sketches (pp. 184–192). Beethoven started it before the first movement was quite finished. We give here the first sketch, from which Beethoven retained only the guitar-like accompaniment in the left hand and a motive for the middle section:

And here is the main melody, which appears somewhat later, in its first version:

The second movement of the G major sonata brings us to the end of the sketchbook.

Apart from the many fascinating musical insights which the sketchbook affords, it also gives a great deal of chronological information. Disregarding for the moment the places where the sketches overlap, and considering only the most important features, we can give the following chronological order for the finished and subsequently published works:

Matthisson's 'Opferlied', first working.
Scene and aria for soprano, 'No, non turbarti'—.
Three of the twelve country dances.
Bagatelle for piano, no. 6 of Op. 33.
Final movement of the D major symphony.
Five of the six Ländler-type dances.
Terzet, 'Tremate, empi, tremate'—Op. 116.
First and second movements of the sonata for piano and violin in A major, Op. 30 no. 1.
Final movement of the sonata for piano and violin in A major, Op. 47.
Sonata for piano and violin in C minor, Op. 30 no. 2.
Bagatelle for piano, no. 5 of Op. 119 (112).
First movement of the piano sonata in D minor, Op. 31 no. 2 (first draft only).
Sonata for piano and violin in G major, Op. 30 no. 3.
Final movement of the sonata for piano and violin in A major, Op. 30 no. 1. (The theme for this was sketched earlier.)

Variations for piano in E-flat major, Op. 35 (preliminary work).
Variations for piano in F major, Op. 34 (first hints only).
Sonata for piano in G major, Op. 31 no. 1 (incomplete).

At the beginning of this essay the period between October 1801 and May 1802 was taken to be the time during which Beethoven wrote in the sketchbook, and we must therefore assign the above listed pieces to that period. We can also make a further deduction, in accordance with the data, about the pieces which are not quite finished in the sketchbook, and assert that the following were completed during the latter half of 1802, partly in Heiligenstadt:

The two piano sonatas in G major and D minor, Op. 31 nos. 1 and 2.[21]
The seven Bagatelles for piano, Op. 33.
The variations in F major, Op. 34.
The variations in E-flat major, Op. 35.
The Symphony in D major, Op. 36.

NOTES

1. The most renowned composers in Vienna were engaged in writing music for the royal balls, including J. Haydn, Mozart and Beethoven himself, whose twelve published minuets and twelve German dances were written, as stated in the advertisement, 'out of affection for the brotherhood of the creative artists' (aus Liebe zur Kunstverwandt-schaft), on the occasion of a ball for exponents of the creative arts, in November 1795. Two years later they were performed again for the same occasion. Other Vienna composers active in this connection between 1795 and 1802 included F. X. Süssmayr, Anton Teyber, Johann Henneberg, von Rossi, A. Höllmayr, Franz Teyber, Joseph Lipavsky, J. Fuchs, Ignaz von Seyfried, Wenzeslaus Pichl, J. Hörmann, J. Adamer, Joseph Eybler etc. The pieces they wrote were, with the exception of a single collection of Ländler by Höllmayr, exclusively minuets and German dances (*Allemandes*). These are also the only dances we find in the advertisements for the balls, so these seem to have been the main dances. At public balls from around 1800 Contretänze and Ländler also figured. These four kinds of dances were probably the most popular for private occasions as well. Since the sketchbook contains dances only of these kinds (apart from the German dances), it is likely that they were all written under commission and for certain specific societies, perhaps for the 'Redouten' or larger private balls, where an orchestra was employed, or perhaps for smaller balls, where as a rule the music was played by two violins and bass (violoncello), or violin and piano, or piano alone.
2. Wegeler ascribed to the song a different text, which he states (*Biographische Notizen* pp. 67 and 69) was written in 1797. Either Wegeler must be mistaken here, or one cannot thereby assume that the song was already composed by then. The second arrangment belongs to a later period; at any rate it seems not to have become known before 1822.
3. Beethoven later wrote disdainfully over the manuscript, 'Esercizii da Beethoven'.
4. It is not certain when the '*Contredances pour 2 Violons et Basse et Instruments à Vent : ad libitum*' (printed by T. Mollo and Co.) first appeared, but there is reason to believe that it was between the middle of 1802 and the middle of 1803. According to an advertisement in the *Wiener Zeitung* of April 3rd 1802 six of them appeared in a piano arrangement (T. Mollo and Co.).

5. The first of the three Contretänze in the sketchbook has elsewhere, in the autograph score, the superscription, 'Contredanse pour Monsieur Friederich, nommé Liederlich'. We cannot be sure whom Beethoven meant by this. It may be conjectured that it was Joh. Bapt. Friederich, the assistant of Dr. J. A. Schmidt, Beethoven's doctor in 1802. Further information on Schmidt may be found in Wegeler's *Notizen*, pp. 39 and 42, in the Heiligenstadt Testament* etc.

6. The seven Bagatelles Op. 33 appeared in the Kunst- und Industrie-Comptoir in Vienna and were first announced in the *Wiener Zeitung* of May 28th 1803. The manuscript submitted for engraving bears, next to the first piece on the first page, the remarkable date 1782. But the manuscript shows that the Bagatelles cannot belong to this year (in which Beethoven was twelve years old); they belong to a later time, approximately that of their publication and of our sketchbook. If there is still some significance to be attached to the date, one may assume that Beethoven used for the work motives and sketches dating from his boyhood.

7. As far as we know, the D major symphony was completed by the autumn of 1802 and was first performed on Shrove Tuesday, April 5th 1803, in the Theater an der Wien.

8. The *Sechs ländlerische Tänze*, doubtless originally composed for two violins and bass, were published by Artaria and Co. and were first announced, together with an arrangement for piano, in the *Wiener Zeitung* of September 11th 1803. (cf. note 1).

9. The Terzet Op. 116 was first performed on February 27th 1814. Beethoven, who on this day gave a 'musikalische Akademie' in the great Redoutensaal, described it in his announcement as 'a quite new, as yet unheard, vocal terzet'. When it was again performed at a similar function in the same place on May 23rd 1824 it was once again announced on the bill as 'new'. In this connection we may refer to a so far unpublished letter. The letter concerns Duport, who was at the time deputising for the director of the Hofoperntheater. (cf. Schindler's biography, vol. II pp. 57 and 73.);** it is addressed to Tobias Haslinger, a partner in the firm of S. A. Steiner and Co. Beethoven writes:

Dear Friend,
You would do me a great injustice, were you to think that it was from remissness that I failed to send you tickets; I certainly did think of it. Like so much else it was forgotten; I hope another opportunity will come for me to show how I do think about you. I am by the way totally innocent in everything Duport has done—passing the Terzet off for

---

*Readily available in English in Emily Anderson's edition of the letters. [Transl.]
**In the modern English edition (*Beethoven as I knew him*) see pp. 237, 271 etc. [Transl.]

new—it was not I that did so. You know only too well my love of truth, but now it is better to keep quiet about it while not everyone knows the truth of the matter and I am not misjudged in my innocence. I have no interest in Duport's other proposals, since this kind of Akademie has merely lost me time and money.

In haste, your friend

Beethoven

Pour Mr. de Haslinger géneral musicien et géneral lieutenant.

Beethoven sold the manuscript of the Terzet to Steiner on April 29th 1815. After its appearance it was quite correctly assessed, in the *Leipziger allgemeine musikalische Zeitung* in July 1826, in respect of its early origin: 'This Terzet is probably from the Master's earlier period—the same period as the well-known great Scena and Aria for soprano. It is conceived, arranged and executed in the manner of the great terzets and quartets in the Opera Seria of that time, just as the aria is conceived, arranged and executed in the manner of the great arias.'

The great Scena and Aria mentioned in this review can be none other than the piece now known as Op. 65, 'Ah perfido'. Beethoven wrote it in 1796 in Prague. This date is on a transcript of the score which is discussed in Schindler's biography (3rd ed. I p. 58).* Since Schindler's statements about this are not quite accurate, or are incomplete, the following observations may serve for correction. The score, written in another hand, was revised by Beethoven and contains corrections throughout in his hand. It has two titles or headings. On the first page Beethoven has written 'Une grande Scene mise en Musique par L. v. Beethoven a Prague 1796', and on the third page 'Recitativo e Aria composta e dedicata alla Signora Contessa di Clari di L. v. Beethoven'. There is no opus number (Op. 46) in Beethoven's hand; it was added by A. Fuchs. In Schönfeld's *Jahrbuch der Tonkunst von Prag*, 1796, p. 120, there is a reference: 'Klary, Josepha Gräfinn, daughter of the late Graf Philipp Excellenz, sings with great charm.'

10. Beethoven put this idea to use in the considerably later piano sonata in C minor, Op. 111. In another sketchbook which contains sketches for this sonata it appears first in a version similar to its original form:

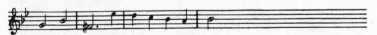

Twenty years must have elapsed between the original conception and the employment of this motive.

11. We know from the same journal (1863, pp. 841 ff.) that Beethoven

Beethoven as I knew him, p. 73. [Transl.]

extracted and copied articles from the *Leipziger allgemeine musikalische Zeitung*.

12. This finds agreement in Ries (*Biographische Notizen*, p. 83), who writes that the final Allegro of the Op. 47 sonata originally belonged to the first A major sonata, Op. 30. He then adds, 'Beethoven later substituted the present variations for this movement, since it was too brilliant for the sonata.' We shall encounter these variations also in the sketchbook.

13. This Bagatelle is found again among later sketches.

14. The sketch bears the title '*Sonate 2*', and certainly the sonata is now the second of a set of three; but at the time when the sketch originated the first of them had not yet been written, as we shall see later. If the title '*Sonate 2*' was not added at a later stage, the only explanation is that the work was originally intended to appear with another sonata, written earlier. This can only be the sonata in D major, Op. 28. According to the autograph it was composed in 1801 and appeared in August 1802. Both dates accord well with what we assumed at the start was the time of the sketchbook. The title '*Sonata 2da*' appears a few times also at the end of the sketchbook.

15. Tradition has it that Beethoven came upon the motive of the last movement when during his time at Heiligenstadt he looked out of the window and saw a rider passing by at a canter. The tradition comes from Czerny, and there is a letter by him to the same effect (cf. *Cocks's musical miscellany*, vol. I, 125). We need not devote time to discussing the authority of such anecdotes.

16. The little grace notes which come in bar 5 of the printed editions appear in the sketches mostly written out in rhythmically exact form. Beethoven may have reverted to the older practice in order to conceal a kind of *mi contra fa* between the upper and lower parts.

17. The original manuscript of the A major sonata Op. 30 no. 1 gives 1802 as the year of composition. (cf. note 12).

18. The Op. 35 variations were ready for the printer in December 1802. Another deduction can be made in this connection. We know that Beethoven used the theme of these variations in three other works, namely *Prometheus*, a collection of Contretänze and in the last movement of the *Sinfonia Eroica*. The question of the chronology of these works has often been raised, but apparently never quite solved. The sketchbook has something to contribute here, since it contains sketches for two of these works (the Contretänze near the beginning and later the variations), whose chronology or order is consequently not in doubt. Now *Prometheus* (first performed in March 1801) belongs to an earlier time than the sketchbook, and the *Sinfonia Eroica* (completed in August 1804) to a later time. This establishes the following chrono-

logical order: 1. *Prometheus* 2. the Contretänze 3. the Op. 35 variations 4. the *Sinfonia Eroica*.

19.   The F major variations Op. 34 were ready for the printer at the end of 1802.

20.   One cannot help remembering here Ries's story (*Biographische Notizen*, p. 88) of the four bars inserted by Naegeli.

21.   The first announcement known to us of the appearance of the G major and also the D minor sonata is dated May 21st 1803. The time of composition or completion can at present be established only indirectly. Ries (*Notizen*, p. 88) tells us that Beethoven was living in Heiligenstadt when the sonatas were about to be sent off. Now Beethoven lived in Heiligenstadt in 1802 roughly from May to October. We know this from a passage in the Testament, which he wrote in October 1802: 'This is how it was over the last half year, which I have spent in the country.' In 1801 Beethoven lived in Hetzendorf and in 1803 in Oberdöbling. We may deduce that these sonatas were ready for the printer by the summer or autumn of 1802. This is supported by a letter written by Beethoven's brother on November 23rd 1802, in which, among other pieces, three piano sonatas, though not yet finished, were offered to the firm of André. Schindler gives the text of the letter (*Biographie* I p. 75).* Carl Czerny said that Beethoven had *composed* the Op. 31 sonatas in Heiligenstadt. If he based this statement on what Ries wrote, we should remember that Ries spoke as an eye-witness and did not say that the sonatas were composed in Heiligenstadt, but simply that they were despatched from there.

The G major and D minor sonatas first appeared in the fifth volume of Naegeli's *Repertoire des Clavecinistes*. Beethoven then sent them, as Ries tells us, (*Notizen*, pp. 89 ff.) to Simrock in Bonn, where they were published as '*Deux Sonates très correctes pour le Pianoforte*, Op. 31'. They were also published (as Op. 29) by J. Cappi in Vienna. It may thus be questionable who of these three should be considered the original publisher. However, Beethoven himself has supplied an answer to this, which at least shows us in what sense he recognised the legitimate claim of a first edition. Around 1815 a Vienna 'Kunstfreund' started a thematic catalogue of Beethoven's works, detailing with conspicuous care the publisher of each work; in this catalogue Beethoven himself gave as the original publisher of the three sonatas Op. 29 (or 31) Naegeli alone, and therewith denied the others this designation.

---

*Beethoven as I knew him, pp. 90 f. Also in the modern English edition of Thayer, p. 314. [Transl.]

A SKETCHBOOK OF 1803

INTRODUCTION

THE ROYAL LIBRARY in Berlin houses a sketchbook which is of quite unusual interest to us.* It dates from a time of profound change in Beethoven's style and in it are to be found almost the entire sketches for a work which is especially relevant for our observation and analysis of the complete transition from one period to another, since it is the most significant work of the time in question. From the evidence offered by the sketches we may draw certain conclusions which can contribute much to the historical study of Beethoven's style and greatly enhance our understanding of his creative work. The very importance of the sketchbook demands at times a detailed treatment in the exposition of such evidence. Scanty extracts are of no use for this purpose; if we are to be able to examine the origins and the evolution of this pre-eminently interesting work, the sketches for a movement or section under scrutiny must be presented as far as possible in complete form and placed in context. An acquaintance must be gained not only with the opening and closing stages of the creative process but also with the intermediate stages through which the work had to pass. The extracts must be sufficient to convince the reader. We cannot here enter into the various conclusions to be drawn from an assessment of the evidence, but later a few words will be said about them.

Our sketchbook is an oblong-folio, 182-page volume with some pages of sixteen staves and some of eighteen. It is properly bound by a bookbinder, is trimmed and has a stiff pasteboard cover; it was already bound in this form when Beethoven began using it. Apart from some seven pages which are left blank and one page written in pencil, it is written entirely in ink. It follows that Beethoven can have used it only indoors. With the exception of five leaves which have been torn out, it has remained as

*This sketchbook, officially referred to now as Landsberg 6, has disappeared, but fortunately survives on microfilm. [Transl.]

complete as when left by the composer. Before page one there is one leaf missing, and four are lacking between pages two and three; from page three onwards our examination of the sketches is unimpeded.

From the dates of some of the compositions worked on in the sketchbook, the greater part, if not all, of the book appears to belong to the year 1803. In attempting to determine the dates more exactly and limit them within certain months, we encounter some difficulties. Most of the dates offered us are either too late, being those of a fair copy or publication of a composition, or are insufficiently certain to be used as a firm basis for argument. We are left vacillating between probability and conjecture. Taking all considerations into account, and assuming that at most nine months can have passed between the writing of the first and last pages, we may say that the sketchbook was used between October 1802 and April 1804.

We need not enter further now into the phenomena which Beethoven's sketchbooks in general present, nor into his working method etc. Enough has been said elsewhere on these matters.* One thing should be remembered, however: there is no doubt that the compositions worked on in a sketchbook were begun in the order in which they appear in the book itself. Nevertheless, the pages were not always filled in their apparent order; when he began a new composition, Beethoven had the habit of starting on a new page and leaving some preceding pages blank for the continuation or completion of a piece he had started earlier. If both compositions were worked on simultaneously or alternately, and for the continuation of the one started later there was no space left, it could happen that pages were used which had previously remained blank, so that eventually the sketches for various compositions became jumbled together. Because of this intermixture of groups of sketches, it cannot always be assumed that those sketches which appear first were in fact written first. One such instance is to be found right at the start of the book.

When there are variant versions in a sketch, these are in the present transcription sometimes given above the places to which they belong, and sometimes appended to the sketch or added later. Their exact points of connection are indicated sometimes

*Vid. 'A Sketchbook of 1802', pp. 4f. above. [Transl.]

by signs, sometimes by the separated syllables of the word 'Vi—de', and sometimes by the word *oder* (or). The *etc.* which sometimes appears in or after a sketch is Beethoven's own. The *u.s.w.* (and so on) marks a sketch which has been shortened in our edition. A question-mark has been placed over those passages where the orthography is in doubt. Accidentals are often missing before notes, and it is left to the reader to supply these. Chronological and biographical information is to be found in the notes at the end of this essay. The reader may also find there a chronological conclusion which we owe to the sketchbook in spite of the otherwise uncertain nature of its chronology. It should also be said that, where in the exposition of the sketches it is necessary to define the aim which Beethoven had or may have had in mind, we shall generally have recourse only to the printed work itself. Speculation would often be hazardous, whereas reference to the score removes any possible ambiguity.

THE SKETCHBOOK

NOW TO THE sketchbook itself. It begins (p. 1) with some sketches for unknown pieces, among them the beginning of a song, 'Zur Erde sank die Ruh' vom Himmel nieder', and (pp. 2, 3, 5) with sketches for the variations for piano on the song 'Rule Britannia'. The latter are of much the same kind as his sketches for other similar sets of variations; first are noted down a number of different motives which are the basis of the variations and are normally to form their openings; then later a part of them is worked out in detail.[1]

In between and directly after these, there appear (pp. 3–10) short, unconnected sketches for the first, second and fourth movements of the *Sinfonia Eroica*; but these were written later than the sketches which immediately follow. We shall have occasion to comment on them below.

The next sketches (pp. 10–41) are concerned almost exclusively with the first movement of the *Sinfonia Eroica*. There is no single sketch covering the whole movement; the longest we have are only for one part of it. For the first part of the movement there are four long sketches, each with variants, and a large number of shorter ones.

Of all the sketches we have, the first of these longer ones, which breaks off shortly before the end of the section, serves best to illustrate the point which Beethoven's work had reached when he started to write in the book:

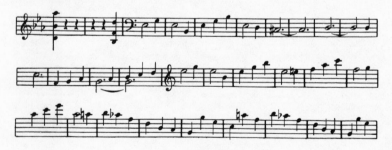

It shows that when it was written the work was already fairly far advanced, and must therefore have been begun elsewhere. It is possible that we have here the very first long, connected sketch for the first part of the movement and that short sketches from an earlier sketchbook are combined in it. In its first half the more important themes and motives are more or less clearly defined. It agrees most closely with the printed version at the beginning of the first subject (bars 3 f.) and in the melody of the first part of the second group (bars 55 f.). The second half, on the other hand, is with the exception of a few motives still far removed. The pattern of modulation is established, as is the sequence of themes and passages, even if in places it is nowhere near the final form.

We shall now follow the changes which the separate parts and components were to undergo. Beethoven later changed the first two bars thus:

These two bars do not appear again in their original or their modified form in the remaining sketches which deal with the beginning of this section; nor for that matter do the two introductory chords of the printed score. So it seems that these were added only after the movement was completed in the sketches.

If we compare the handling of the principal subject in the two versions, we find that in the sketch the third statement of the theme is in B-flat major, whereas in the score it remains in E-flat major. But a variant to the sketch (on p. 10) shows a correspondence to the published version:

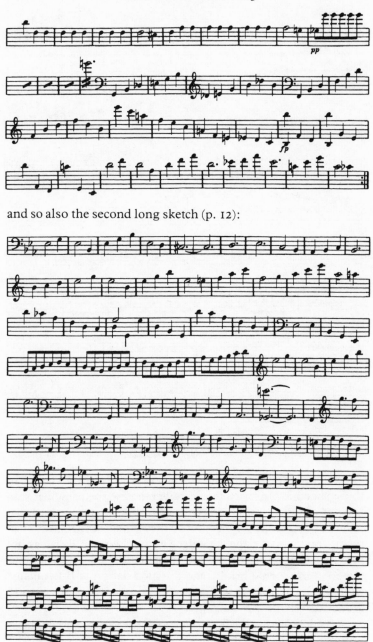

and so also the second long sketch (p. 12):

However, Beethoven did not remain on the path started in these sketches. In two sketches given below the principal subject comes four times, and the fourth time it is again in B-flat major. The reason for Beethoven's eventual return after such repetition, and after the statement of the theme in B-flat, is not hard to surmise. A three-fold presentation was sufficient to establish the theme firmly, and the modulation to B-flat major would simply have weakened the ensuing entry of the second group melody in the same key.

There appeared in the first four bars of the variant shown above a motive which (with the tenth note lengthened) was later to be

54

employed in the second part of the movement, and by which within the otherwise rather relaxed first subject an element of contrast was achieved. In the third long sketch (pp. 14 f.)

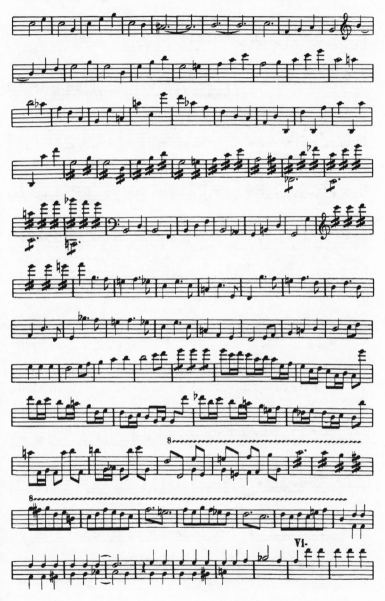

this motive appears in modified form but still with its $^2/_4$ pulse. This very effective syncopation is found also in the fourth long sketch (pp. 20 f.):

57

The first subject can herewith be considered essentially complete. The book presents no more sketches which can be linked with it.

In the first long sketch (bars 43–54) and its variants the transition from first subject to 'second group'* appeared still in incomplete form and with a motive principally in crotchets. In the second long sketch it assumed what was to become its basic rhythmic character. Beethoven may have found it unsatisfactory in the earlier version because, with its notes of equal value, it did not seem capable of separating sufficiently the principal subject and the first part of the second group, both containing crotchet notes. With the different treatment of the tune in the third and fourth long sketches the final form is first approached and then fully attained in its essentials.

As these sketches show, the melody of the first part of the second group required few changes before the final form was reached. But the passage which leads from it to the second part of the second group took longer to find the bold line and the expansion in which we know it. Much remained to be done to it as it appeared in the first long sketch (bars 59 f.). It should be noticed that in almost all the workings on this passage, however different they may be from the first sketch, the rhythmic character as found in that sketch is preserved; the arrangement of the motive differs in the second long sketch from that in the first, but the passage has not yet taken flight. This and other faults hamper a few smaller sketches, here omitted. It is in the third and fourth long sketches that the printed version is most closely approached,

*German 'Seitensatz' (*vid.* translator's note p. vii above). [Transl.]

except that in the third some work remained to be done on the end of the passage and in the fourth the urgent forward movement, which is so characteristic of, and essential to, the passage right from its inception, is arrested in the middle by the repetition of a bar.

The quaver movement of the second part of the second group in the first long sketch has been replaced in the variant to that sketch by a crotchet passage. In this variant the theme consists of two four-bar sections. In the second long sketch the sections of the theme have been lengthened, and in the third sketch the theme is extended to three and more sections. We can notice here the composer's striving for expansion. In the third long sketch the expansion occurs principally through repetition. The first four-bar section returns as the third in the higher octave. This repetition is ungrounded, or at least unnecessary. The theme, so simple in its repeated crotchet pattern, seems to call for transformation rather than mere repetition. What it contained could be sufficiently expressed in two four-bar sections. An effective reiteration of the theme could be produced if it appeared in a different colouring, and such a change in colouring could be achieved by transposition to the tonic minor key. This is just what happens in a variant to the third long sketch (p. 15):

(The context reveals that the key of the opening here is B-flat minor.) From this point on the repetition of the theme always comes in B-flat minor, and because of this modification the way to a new version was now open.

Several of the subsequent sketches (on pp. 15–18) are concerned with rendering differently the shape of the languid, mournful F minor passage into which the B-flat minor theme leads in this variant (bar 12) and which also occurs in another place and in a different form in the third long sketch. The last of these sketches is given here (p. 18):

The fourth long sketch shows that Beethoven then abandoned the passage and found in the theme itself material with which to develop it. In this way, especially by the use of its rhythmic motive, the subject gains in cohesion and strength.

There follow just a few more sketches which quickly approach the final form as we know it. So on pp. 22 and 23:

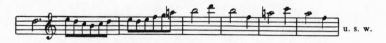

Here the first four bars of the subject have found their final form. In the next example (p. 26) the theme, which in its previous versions could more appropriately be called a succession of melodic fragments than a true melody, has acquired a firm and regular periodic shape:

These last sketches occasion a few remarks. In the variant to the last sketch above, the final section (bars 1–9), into which the B-flat minor passage is resolved, up to the quaver passage leading to the end-section, is formed from two motives taken from the second part of the second group— ♪♪♪│♩♪ and ♪♪♩ . One should notice that the first of these consists of three notes of the same pitch and a descending second. In the final score the passage appears somewhat differently:

61

The movement of the melody is here broken twice by slurred notes of different pitch. The passage gains an elegance and beauty through this modification—through the abandonment of a strictly 'motivic' treatment—and consequently the following second motive enters in its hesitant rhythm with greater effect. The above sketch should provide a commentary, as it were, on the printed reading; the latter is not found in the sketchbook, and we can conclude that it originated later.

The second observation brings us back to the first long sketch. Of all the extant sketches this is the one in which we can see the first conception of this section of the movement and which represents most faithfully the composer's original idea. However dissimilar it may be to the final version, it still contains some features which survive in different guise in the score we know. We need merely recall the two introductory bars which occur in this sketch alone and then not again until their re-appearance with a different content in the full score. Following the modulation in the score one notices that the most distant key touched on is D-flat major, and it is in the second part of the second group that the music turns towards this key. In the sketches which immediately follow there is no noticeable effort to reach this key, though the effort is certainly evident in later sketches; we need only examine the two last sketches given above (from pp. 22, 23 and 26 of the book), in which the modulation to D-flat major occurs in the same position as in the first sketch, and in which furthermore this is the only remote key reached in the course of the exposition. Though an immediate connection between the original and final versions cannot here be conclusively proven, nevertheless this agreement in modulation is remarkable. If there is anything 'prophetic' to be ascribed to the first sketch, then the modulatory idea established in it may be considered realized in changed form in the final score.

The nearer we come to the end of the exposition, the more numerous become the sketches. Most numerous of all are those for the closing section; indeed because of the diversity of material we find, it is difficult not to lose the main thread.

In the first long sketch and its variant, the end-section*
(assuming that is what we can call the section following the
second part of the second group) appears as a combination and
sequential development of several motives, with no firm tonal
body until the closing phrase itself towards the end of the section
and the principal subject which follows it. Otherwise the only
viable material to appear in the development of the end-section
was a short zigzag passage in quavers and the passage-like**
extension of the third bar of the principal subject. (Under the
quaver passage, which in the variant follows the second part of the
second group, is to be supplied a bass part formed from the third
bar of the principal subject.) The formation of the second part of
the second group could not fail to influence that of the end-
section. This is already to be seen in the second long sketch.
Here the second part of the second group is more extended and
more definite in content, while the end-section is similarly more
extended and employs a greater variety of thematic material. The
chromatic end of the second part of the second group gives it a
melancholic character. It seems almost to express a sad remi-
niscence on the departed hero. This chromatic passage urged
forward towards something of firm substance; what better to
counteract it than the principal subject (as in the second
sketch)—the 'heroic' motive itself, which now enters, *pianis-
simo*, as if comforting and softly stirring.

Beethoven evidently spent some time on basing the end-
section predominantly on the principal subject and on parts of it.
One can see this in several sketches, in which however the
principal subject is introduced not in B-flat major (as in the
second sketch) but in E-flat major, first in this fragment (p. 11)—

*Germ. 'Schlusspartie'. (*Vid.* translator's note.)
**The German 'ganghaft' and 'gangartig', used liberally by Nottebohm
over the next few pages, are difficult to translate by a single English
term. The implication is one of a 'transitional' passage—'*Gang*'—
always leading on to something else, as opposed to a self-contained
musical phrase. [Transl.]

63

then in the third long sketch, and then in the following (p. 16):

The parts of the principal subject employed in this and other sketches and used as passages* are sometimes the third and fourth bars and sometimes the third bar alone. (Here again a bass part formed from this material can be considered to underlie the syncopated notes following in the treble clef after the restatement of the principal subject in the third long sketch.)

*'gangartig', see footnote above. [Transl.]

We must now give the last-quoted sketch some thought. This sketch, which must be seen as following the second part of the second group in the version in which it leads into a chromatic passage as in the second long sketch, is the first in which three passage-like* melodic sections appear, formed from different motives; these survive in the same order, though differently expressed, in the full score. They are as follows, though they underwent constant change until they reached their final version: 1. a descending and rising passage in quavers; 2. a passage formed principally from the motive | ♩ ♩ ♩ |; 3. repeated chords in the ²/₄ rhythm | ♩ ♩ ♩ | ♩ ♩ ♩ |. The basic figure underlying the quaver passage is already to be found in the first long sketch, but does not then reappear until the above sketch. The basic motives of the other two elements apparently occur here for the first time. The origin of the first of them might be sought in the theme of the second part of the second group, were it not for the appearance of a few small sketches, e.g. (p. 14)

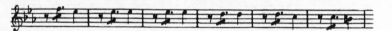

and the fact that the motive used in the end-section has a step of a second, while the basic motive of the second part of the second group in all sketches before this one remains on the same note. So these two elements would seem here to have an individual origin. Examining the sketch as a whole, we find the principal subject, woven in as a passage figure* (in E-flat major) and flanked by transpositions of its third and fourth bars. It passes us by like a vision; there is something nebulous about this transition from second group to end-section. The sketch was obviously capable of demonstrating clearly that such a transition—a continual succession of passages formed from different motives and figures—was not sufficient to display in suitable light the end-section, similarly constructed in a succession of passages, with all its powerful motives and its buoyancy and vigour; a proper relation between the two sections, so rich and so different in content, could be established only by placing a separating element between them. The 'partition' had to rest on

*'gangartig', see footnote above. [Transl.]

a basis of secure tonality, and this had to be B-flat major; furthermore what belonged on this basis was not a transitional passage,
nor a tentative theme, entering softly, but a theme of marked
rhythm entering decisively.

And so Beethoven's task now is to find a new and independent
theme to open the final section. In attempting to find this theme
he uses his previous material only in so far as, amongst the ten or
so themes which are found, e.g. on p. 4

and on p. 18

he presents once in a variant (the beginning of which was quoted
above on p. 60 of this treatise) a theme formed from the first two
bars of the principal subject:

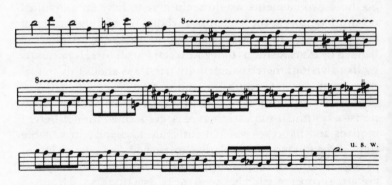

In comparison with the themes conceived first, those that
came later have steps of wider intervals and are consequently
more vigorous in character. The reason for this can be found in
the gradual formation of the second part of the second group,

which, because of its melancholic colouring and the concentration it acquired in time, came to demand an end-section with a powerful and energetic opening to follow. Beethoven had in the meantime started work on the second part of the movement, and here the principal subject was to be used in development. In working on the start of the end-section he was surely influenced not only by the constantly changing second part of the second group, but also by the reflection that it was inadvisable to anticipate this imminent statement of the principal subject.

With the presentation of a clearly defined theme the work now entered a new phase. A focal point had developed, into which the lines from two different directions had to converge, and which in turn could not remain without influence on both of these lines. In general, the difference between the sketches which now follow and the earlier ones is an increasing attention to gaining maximum variety of content. The procedure is now the opposite of that observed in the sketches for the second part of the second group, which, considered in their sequence, show more and more limitation in the choice of material, though not in its treatment; the motives chosen for development are ultimately taken from the theme itself, whereas in the sketches for the end-section the opening theme is not used for motivic development, and other, new themes are adduced. The aim was to use the presentation of different 'images', successively supplanting each other, to counterbalance the composite nature of the second part of the second group—in other words, to give the end-section the force and energy which the second part of the second group lacked. For the moment the interweaving of individual parts of the principal subject is disregarded, and the three elements we saw in an earlier sketch (taken from page 16 of the sketchbook) now comes to the fore.

It would be a mistake to assume that Beethoven was on a straight path to the final version once he had found the three important elements of the end-section and decided on the presentation of a special opening theme. On the contrary, there were still problems to overcome. We shall concentrate for the moment on the more important aspects. There is little progress to be seen in one of the following sketches—i.e. the first longer one in which the end-section appears with an independent theme at its opening (p. 18):

or in this next one, the beginning of which was shown above (on p. 60 of this treatise):

The passages written here after the repeated opening theme (with or without variation) lack power and fluency, chiefly because the music remains in one harmonic position. What was to follow depended on the formation of this first passage. In the fourth long sketch, which soon follows, a new motive is introduced. In its development in a variant to the sketch (p. 21) it turns out to be a part of the principal subject:

Beethoven thus seems to have reverted to an earlier idea, for this motive is basically the same as that which played a part in the earlier sketches for the end-section but was then abandoned. Now the motive is taken up again. The following sketch, in which it does not appear, is an exception (p. 22):

But this sketch comes noticeably close to the final version. In bars 9–25 the three 'elements' which have concerned us have been developed and have reached their final form. The first passage is an exception, being longer in the sketch than in the printed version, but this difference is not an essential one; it is more significant that this passage, with its constant upward movement, has now acquired its harmonic change at every crotchet and therewith the power to introduce effectively the subsequent syncopated crotchet beats interrupted by crotchet rests. However the material here conceived was still not finally secure, and Beethoven searched on.

In our next extract and its variant the motive passed over in the previous sketch is taken up again, but by abbreviation it produces the third bar of the principal subject (p. 26).

This, with a change in the position of the motive, lays open the way to the final version. The pre-eminently important feature of the score is the sudden interruption, by the motive taken from the principal subject and rising alone from the depths, of the syncopated, as it were mutually opposing chords separated by crotchet rests. We may well wonder whether Beethoven would ever have arrived at this without all the various preceding attempts at employing the principal subject, or parts of it, in the end-section.

Another aspect should be mentioned. In the last sketches, to vary the opening theme of the end-section, Beethoven has used the figure with which the subsequent passage begins. Because the passage appears as an offshoot of the modified theme, the beginning of the end-section up to the entry of the crotchets presents itself as a thematically coherent whole. This cohesion is not found in the final score; certainly the opening theme is varied, but in such a way that the passage appears without thematic connection to what precedes it. Beethoven must have had his reasons for abandoning the version in the sketch; perhaps it was because the decisiveness with which the end-section was to begin was better matched by the longer, incisive marcato notes of the printed version than by the quavers in this variation.

After this sketch there follow some of less significance which can be passed over here. With these we come to the end of the sketches for the exposition.

To the second part (development section) of the movement belong many short sketches and two which extend over the whole section. Here, as elsewhere, a part of the shorter sketches is incorporated in the longer ones.

It can be seen from the first short sketches that before Beethoven had done any other work on the second part of the movement he had decided on the lyrical episode in E minor, and also on its entry in that key. This dictated the direction, if not the complete course, of the modulation it needed; it had at any rate to be a far-reaching one.

It was soon established also that shortly before the end of the section the principal subject should enter in the tonic below an echo of the dominant seventh. The reason for this assertion is to be found in a sketch right at the beginning of the book (on p. 4):

The *cumulus** occurs here and is conclusive evidence that Beethoven conceived this special feature long before the basic character of the second part of the movement was established. But he also sought other more or less strange ways of introducing the recapitulation. We can learn something of the history of this passage from the following extracts from the shorter sketches, given here in the order in which they appear; more will be given later.

*This is the standard continental term for the famous horn entry that precedes the recapitulation. [Transl.]

In this sketch (p. 30) Beethoven has hit on the idea of presenting the principal subject, shortly before the beginning of the
recapitulation, in the remote key of D major; but the appended
variant shows that he then changed his mind. A possible, though
perhaps unlikely, reason is that a modulatory effect was to be
used shortly after this point—that is to say at the beginning of
the recapitulation, where the theme enters first in E-flat major
and then in F major—and this effect would have been weakened
by the earlier passage. In the above variant the dissonance at the
entry of the principal theme is harsher than in the printed version. Beethoven returns to the same dissonance in a later sketch;
this indicates that such a combination was more than a passing
whim and that the composer did at least consider this type of
transition to the recapitulation. On p. 32

and on p. 33

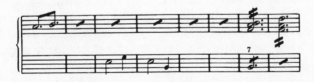

and also in other sketches the original version of the *cumulus*,
with a few modifications, is taken up again. On page 35:

a run takes the place of the *cumulus*. This too was soon rejected. In sketches following soon after (cited below) Beethoven adopts again the *cumulus* and develops it. He does not abandon it again after this.

So we have before us three different types of transition to the recapitulation. If the composer hesitated in choosing between them, it cannot have been for long. It is also to be remarked that no sketch appears which indicates a fourth type of transition on which could be based a replacement for the *cumulus*—a substitution of consonant notes for the dissonant ones etc., as has recently been suggested and attempted. There can be no doubt that Beethoven wrote these bars quite deliberately; the peculiarity of the passage, and the fact that it was planned right at the start, confirm the view that Beethoven was here realizing an intention, and a symbolic significance is to be attributed to it. It is in this very deliberateness that we can find an explanation for the passage.

Of the above-mentioned two long sketches for the development section only the first need be quoted in full, since the second (pp. 38 f.) agrees essentially with the printed version apart from a few passages which we mention below. The first appears on pp. 34 f.:

75

If we compare this sketch with the score, we find that the two meet at six points and diverge in between. Most of the subsequent sketches are concerned with the places of divergence. We shall now follow these workings.

In bar 12 of the sketch Beethoven has the first bars of the principal subject enter in C minor. In the second long sketch the principal idea is reached fourteen bars later and is preceded by the transitional idea from the beginning of the exposition. A possible reason for the change is that the beginning of the principal subject had already been introduced shortly before the end of the exposition, and because of this proximity a more forceful intervening passage was required than that offered by the episode (here right at the beginning of the development section) which stayed mainly in the dominant of C minor. This transitional idea could most justifiably be used here, since of all the themes so far introduced it had remained the longest unused; furthermore it was well suited by its bright major tonality to emphasize effectively the following C minor entry of the main theme.

The fourteen bars preceding the E minor melody in the above sketch were modified on p. 38:

and on p. 39:

If we compare these versions in the order in which they arose and then look at the full score, which contains the final version, we notice that the dissonances grow sharper and that the rhythms become gradually more incisive and begin to run against the beat. Clearly Beethoven's object was to achieve a contrast to the introduction of the elegiac melody—to stress, as it were, the dark blue of this melody by means of a dazzling glare before it.

The melody of the episode, which comes in later in E-flat minor, receives a different treatment on p. 38 from that in the first long sketch:

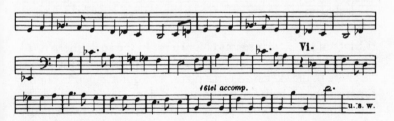

The modulation here is from A-flat minor to G-flat major, and in touching on this key the sketch acquires some similarity to the printed version. What is lacking, however, is the immediate step in the score from E-flat minor to G-flat major and the beautiful entry then following of the initial motive on the subdominant (C-flat) of the latter key.

We do find this entry in a variant to the last sketch above (on p. 39)

though it is weakened by the preceding A-flat minor. And so we have one more feature in the score (where A-flat minor is omitted) which was arrived at only after long consideration.

The following sketch for the end of the second part of the movement (from p. 31) is the first in which the *cumulus* appears together with motives which survive in the score.

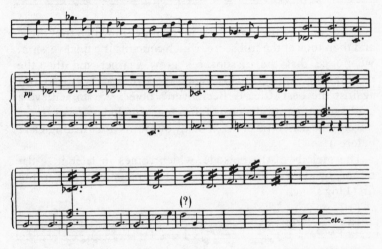

In itself the sketch seems colourless. In the score there is, so to speak, a mountain range between the episode and the *cumulus*; here in the sketch all is flat plain. The quiet, solemn, almost funereal chords between the episode and the *cumulus* provide no more than a harmonic connection between these two equally *piano* subjects and are not suited to prepare an effective entry for the *cumulus*. Beethoven was to show here his gift for colouring. There was insufficient light, and the dark colours had to be emphasized by brighter ones. The *cumulus* had to be illuminated with reflections which would distinguish it as a 'shadow'. A mere transition was not enough. There had to be an intermediate passage with significant dynamic rising and falling, the former to separate and throw into relief the two passages on either side, the latter to prepare the entry of the principal theme and the wonderful harmonic combination. It took few steps to achieve this aim. Already in the first long sketch above one can observe a striving for shading and contrast. A powerful passage, in which we can assume a *crescendo* and *forte*, is inserted, and with it the calm is interrupted by a certain movement.

In the sketch on p. 38 the marvellous bass-movement is stated for the first time and the former vagueness is at an end:

The most important element is now found. In this sketch we also encounter the quaver run which appeared earlier. Beethoven's reason for removing it was clearly that the run would have disturbed the calm which was to precede the *cumulus*.

In a variant to this sketch on p. 39

the run is replaced by four new bars which take up and continue the somewhat arrested movement. With this variant the final version is reached in all its essentials.

While Beethoven was working on the development section he wrote down also the fine F major entry of the principal subject at the start of the third part (recapitulation) of the movement and drafted the first lines for the coda. The coda has several small sketches and three longer ones. The latter are very different from each other. Strikingly, in the first of them (p. 30) the principal subject does not appear in complete form. In the second it is complete, and, as in the full score, only in this form (p. 37):

This sketch agrees with the printed version also in containing the themes which occurred longest before it, namely the bass melody from the development section and the themes of the episode and the first part of the second group. However the course of the modulation and the order in which they are placed are different.

The greater extension of the second sketch—more than 130 bars, as opposed to the 80 of the first sketch—is to be attributed to an effort to achieve thematic completeness. The sketch which follows on p. 41 (but may have been written before the former of these two) is shorter still and is remarkable in presenting a quite new motive and not having the principal theme in full. But in an effort to gain fullness, unity and consistency this sketch was completely suppressed. And so we come to the end of the sketches for the first movement.

While working on the first movement of the symphony Beethoven took the initial steps for the second and third movements.

Apart from the middle subject in C major the Funeral March emerged in fragments. The first subject had to be conquered almost bar by bar. The earliest stage of the work can best be observed in the following sketch (p. 6 of the sketchbook):

The second section here begins with a motive that was later used in a different place in the same section and was treated differently. Some of the features here which seem quite strange to us give way to more familiar traits in the following sketch (p. 42):

Structurally the melody has here gained in clarity and power. Looked at as a whole, and apart from a few divergencies, this is also the first sketch in which the various motives employed appear in the order they have in the final version. Nevertheless, in its details its formulation had a long way yet to go. The composer now begins to work at these finer points, and there are few bars which are not reworked and transformed. So on p. 43:

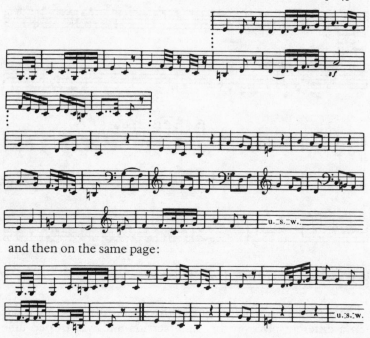

and then on the same page:

and finally on p. 49 the following sketch, with its many alterations, of which only about half is given here:

Of the various transformations we find here, particularly interesting are those concerning bar 8 of the principal theme; we can see that Beethoven was undecided as to whether the cadence should be a suspension, or continue in march rhythm, or perhaps take some other form.

It was soon decided that a fugato should be introduced, and three different themes are presented for this treatment (pp. 9, 42 and 52):

Beethoven writes on p. 48:

Nach der ersten Wiederholung, welche nur in einem Minore - Theil besteht, folgt* — *Inzwischen noch einmal:***

*After the first repeat, which consists only of one *Minore,* comes:
**meanwhile once again:

According to this remark, the second of the three themes above was to enter on the last note of the principal subject, and the middle subject (in the major) or a part of it was to follow the fugato. Later he writes (p. 52):

For this the third theme was chosen, and the principal subject was to follow in C minor immediately after the fugato. This primitive introduction of the first subject was shortly followed by attempts at different types of entry. A marvellous passage arises out of these attempts; we have two sketches in which, after a fugato constructed on the third theme, the beginning of the melody of the principal subject comes in G minor.

In the first of these two, on p. 53, the beginning of which is here omitted, the G minor melody rises by degrees up to A-flat and then leads down immediately into the principal subject in C minor:

This is a purely melodic interlude, which is interrupted in a variant to the sketch:

The note A-flat is held, transferred to the low octave, and the basses, as if about to announce an imminent catastrophe, lead off into a vigorous triplet passage which returns upwards and into the theme. The second sketch is essentially no different from this variant. Beethoven later used the passage as countersubject to the theme entering in another part, instead of leading it into the main theme; but this is only to be seen in the score. Would Beethoven have come to write this passage as it is, had he not been confronted with the A-flat by his attempt to introduce the theme melodically?

Another interlude—the transition from the major-key section to the return of the principal subject—was similarly discovered during a digression, though in the score it seems as if it could never have been other than as it is. To start with, the two sections were to be connected by a passage of the simplest kind which merely filled out the close of the major-key section. This is clear from a sketch on p. 50 (given here from the third bar from the end of that section):

In later sketches, such as our next examples (pp. 51 and 53), which begin on the final note of the major-key section, extra bars are inserted and the passage is displaced by transitions of a predominantly melodic nature:

These constitute the first step towards the final version, which is not to be found in the sketchbook. If it was Beethoven's intention to give the Funeral March melody a significant preparation by inserting a short interlude, he cannot have regarded the versions in the sketchbook as adequate, since the entry would have been weakened by their preponderant C minor tonality. He must have come to prefer the version we know because in it the principal key is F minor, which is particularly suitable for modulating from the clarity of the major section to the relative gloom of the minor-key first subject, and also because there is less digression than, for instance, in the last of the sketches above.

The close of the Funeral March was drafted in the most diverse ways. About eight drafts (pp. 42, 52 etc.) appear in the book. In the first of them the end is reached some eighteen bars earlier than in the version we know. Later sketches, e.g. that on p. 61, the first half of which survives in the score with a few modifications,

show some effort towards expansion. It is in the very last one that Beethoven has the idea of leading to a close by breaking up the metre of the main theme (p. 92):

So in beginning the composition he cannot have been thinking of the symbolic significance which is often attached to this coda.

In all this we have passed over the sketches for the major-key section, since there is nothing especially noteworthy in them. If we consider the Funeral March sketches as a whole, we must conclude that, once the work was under way, the constituent parts of the movement developed in the order in which they appear in the full score. The same is apparently true of the sketches for the third movement.

We find in a fragment on p. 10 the first attempt at the Scherzo of the symphony:

This beginning is taken further (though from the second bar onwards it departs somewhat from the earlier sketch) on p. 36:

The letter M found over both sketches stands for *Menuetto*. So Beethoven intended to write a minuet after the fashion of those in earlier compositions, or at least a minuet-type movement. There is quite a gulf between the minuet in this last sketch and the Scherzo of the Third Symphony; there is a striking difference

89

between the two pieces in the tempo they demand, in length and in general character. There was no step-by-step progress from this stage; Beethoven had reached a point from which a transformation had to take place in one leap. On p. 42 he writes:

and on p. 60:

He has found here the rocking figuration on B-flat and C of the opening motive which contributes so essentially to the scherzo character, or rather is its definitive feature. Progress was fast from this point on; the second section quickly grew in extension, so that in a sketch shortly after this (on p. 66) it has as many bars as in the printed version. From its various sketches we shall now select those which concern the re-entry of the first theme over the pedal-like dominant of E-flat major. The powerful effect and the significance of this passage seem to be due to two features. First, there is the originality of the leap from the dominant of G minor to the mediant of the same key, and the entry of the theme in the six-four position; secondly, a change from one key to another is contained in the repeated note which prepares the re-entry of the opening theme. We must examine the developments which preceded the finding of these combined effects. There are five different versions before us; the object in all of them is to introduce the theme with a pedal-type part. The first three versions have three different ways of re-introducing the theme (pp. 60, 61 and 64):

(These extracts begin at the eighth bar before the theme returns.)
In the first version it comes above the principal motive held like a
pedal point on the dominant of E-flat major; in the second it is on
the bass E-flat; in the third it is even underneath the repeated
note. In none of them, however, is the pedal point part in any key
other than B-flat or E-flat major.

The modulation to G minor takes place for the first time in this
sketch (p. 66):

The entry of the theme follows, either above the principal
motive pattern on the dominant of this key, or, as at the
beginning of the movement, above the bass E-flat; in the sketch

it is not clear which. If it is the first, the modulation at the return of the theme would be similar to the beginning of the recapitulation in the first movement of the D major quartet Op. 18 no. 3. In a variant to this sketch (on p. 67) all the effective moments occur at last together:

Beethoven later removed the crotchets in the upper part at bars 9, 10, 13 and 14 in this sketch, and changed the *ff* of bar 13 to *pp*; therewith the final version was essentially complete. Altogether the sketches show a striving for conciseness and demonstrate that Beethoven did not want a conventional introduction for the theme.

As soon as the minuet became a scherzo, the original trio was no longer acceptable. Beethoven made repeated attempts at a new trio. We find three different drafts, of which none bears any relation to the printed version. We have already seen the beginning of the first of these drafts (from p. 42 of the sketchbook). It is only with the fourth of them (p. 65) that we approach the final form:

It should be noticed that in all of these last sketches Beethoven was intending the three horns to take a dominant role. The contrary was the case with the minuet he rejected; there the horns were to be used in the minuet itself and not in the trio. From the outset, then, Beethoven appears to have intended to employ the horns prominently in the third movement.

The second part of the Trio gave some trouble. In the draft in the above extract and then in the following sketch (p. 65), which is notable for its difference from the printed form in the relation between the two phrases of the first part, and also for the appearance of a later horn-passage, the beginning of the second part is made up of eight-bar sections:

This is a structure which puts the second part in an unfavourable relation to the first, which with its two phrases is similarly in eight-bar sections. Though in some subsequent sketches such uniformity is avoided, with four- and two-bar phrases at the beginning of the second part, they do not come noticeably near to the final version in the motives they use. In looking for an

93

explanation for the origin of the final version we should note another feature of the above sketch: between bars 16 and 24 of the second part there is a passage formed from two-bar phrases. This passage survives in similar shape in the full score. It is striking that the rhythmic accent falls on different bars in the two versions; in the sketch it is at the beginning of the even-numbered bars (counting from the start of the Trio), whereas in the score it falls on the odd-numbered bars. We might perhaps explain both the shift of accent and the origin of the final version if we assume that later in the sketch Beethoven made the second part start one bar earlier, removed from it bars 2, 4, 6, 10, 12 and 14, and compressed bars 7–8 and 15–16 into single bars.

The composition of the last movement took less time than that of the others. Right at the start of his work on it, Beethoven was on the whole decided as to the choice of the theme and the form of the movement. On p. 70 he writes as follows (and this is the first sketch):

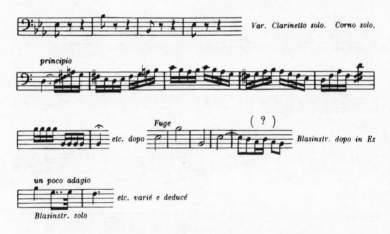

According to this sketch the movement should start with an introductory passage beginning on the dominant of G minor; the bass theme was first to be unaccompanied, and then given variations and fugue; later there should be a slower section with the melody of the theme in the upper part, and so on. This is roughly the course of the printed score.

Beethoven returned repeatedly to the introductory passage (pp. 71 ff.). The last time is on p. 79:

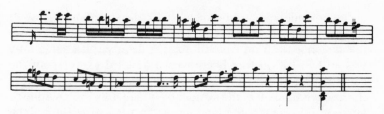

The versions of this section are all different, but all have the common feature of beginning on the dominant of G minor and reaching the dominant of E-flat major. The direction of this modulation is the same as in the second half of the Scherzo at the re-entry of the theme. The difference is that in the Scherzo the change of key is effected in a single step, whereas in the Finale it is spread over a modulatory passage. The possibility of influence between the two is not to be excluded, since the sketches for both are not far separated and must have been written within a fairly short space of time.

The remaining sketches are mostly of a contrapuntal nature. They are concerned with the variations, the fugato, with forming strettos of the bass theme, and so on. Of special interest is the G minor middle section in its original version (p. 71):

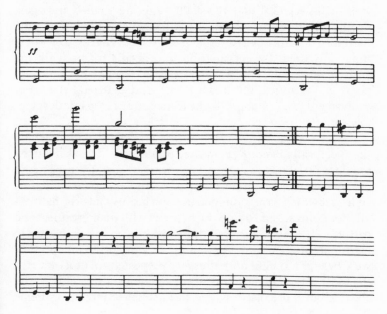

Our consideration of the sketches for the symphony is now at an end. Many passages have not yet found their final version in the sketchbook, from which it may be deduced that some time was still to pass before Beethoven proceeded to work out the composition in full score.[2] Having examined these early stages in the development of the symphony we are now in a position to attempt to bring together and set out in a few observations the most important deductions that can be drawn from our evidence. It is not necessary now to refer to the individual passages on which the following conclusions are based, for it is to be assumed that the reader has ready to hand all the evidence of the sketchbook given above.

Our observations are threefold.

1. On the whole, apart from certain single passages to which from the start attention was drawn and which were held up, as it were, as a yard-stick, not only the movements of the symphony, but also their constituent parts and the individual sections of these parts, were formed and completed in the order in which they appear in print. In spite of his characteristic procedure of working piecemeal and repeatedly altering drafted passages, Beethoven nevertheless constantly had an aim in view and his thoughts were directed towards an entirety, even if the aim was at times obscured. By his entering into details in his work the entirety emerged. What was in process of formation was dependent on the formation of what surrounded it, and the latter evolved out of and along with the former; this is organic development in the truest sense.

2. The *Sinfonia Eroica* ranks as the first major work in which the specifically Beethovenian style broke forth. The sketchbook provides proof that, with very few exceptions, all those passages in the score which bear the stamp of Beethoven's own invididual style and which have combined in them beauty and originality—all those phrases and traits which, partly with their greatness and partly with their warmth, inspire us, shatter us, move us to tears—all of them were far from the creation of a moment; they were brought to light only after many repeated attempts and, for the most part, at the expense of considerable effort. This is true above all of those places where an established motive or theme

was to be developed, realized or worked out. It is towards this kind of development that the majority of the sketches are directed, and it is very striking that the first sketches have in themselves little or even nothing at all of Beethoven's peculiar style and individuality; in fact they are often very ordinary and conventional. And yet they are, as it were, the soil in which the seemingly insignificant took root and bore fruit. An exception is found in those passages which one might call individual or original but perhaps not beautiful—those which have even been called eccentricities or quirks; in this category would be, for instance, the famous horn passage shortly before the recapitulation of the first movement, or the opening in a remote key of the final movement.

3. Attention has been drawn (I believe first by Marx*) to the consistency and rationality which is dominant in Beethoven's works. Observations made in this regard have led to an irrefutable conclusion. The sketchbook convinces us that Beethoven was always conscious of the law, above the ideal which hung before him, of an intrinsic necessity in form; throughout the lengthy process of creation he was compelled to practise an aesthetic critique, and even with continually changing material he had to set about his task with utter consistency. As concerns the outcome, this latter statement is apparently a logical consequence of the former; according to preference, the one may be taken as premise or inference of the other. Therefore it may appear unnecessary to appeal to the sketchbook at all. However, there is a difference between one statement which is deduced from another and a statement which is based on its own particular evidence; also there is a difference between acquainting oneself with this evidence, together with the contingencies and circumstances which are connected with it, and not doing so. The sketchbook gives more precise information than the score can give, namely what kind of agency it was through which that consistency was achieved. In the course of this exposition we have often enough been concerned with this agency, though it was never named; the question now is how to give it the right name. For this purpose it is sufficient to recall one piece of evidence which often recurs. In those sketches which were

*The reference here is to the work of Adolph Bernard Marx (1795–1866). [Transl.]

directed towards developing and shaping already conceived themes or individual ideas—and, as already mentioned, most of the sketches belong to this category—it is beyond doubt that Beethoven always ensured that passages were properly related to one another. From this it is abundantly clear that Beethoven reflected rationally, and the force which he brought to bear was the reflective intellect. Reflection alone, however, is frigid; it is not creative and is incapable of yielding beauty. It cannot be, and is not, the first quality in art. In Beethoven the first quality, and indeed the last, was the creative imagination, but one which had 'passed through' reflection. We must still try to explain how these two opposite forces could be united to work to a common aim. Both forces worked separately and alternately. The conscious and the unconscious were combined. While the intellect examined, sorted and intimated defects, the creative power supplied the demands of the intellect, and in this way established its own freedom of movement and therewith its mastery; it was immune to every restrictive influence that could threaten its being. In most humans the creative faculty grows slack during work, but with Beethoven it was otherwise, for in him it worked on unimpaired; indeed it often rose to its greatest heights only at the last moment. This flexibility of creativity and intellectual rigour, controlled, considered and steadfastly patient, goes to make up one part of the qualities on which Beethoven's greatness rested and without which Beethoven would never have been Beethoven; but one part only, for there were other contributary qualities, which can, with some reservation in regard to the properties above attributed to the creative imagination, be summarised by the word 'genius'. There is a difference between the two classes of qualities; the latter are inborn faculties, whereas the former are acquired and are to be ascribed not to the individual and nature but rather to the personality and character; it is these qualities whose influence is at work in an evident manner in the sketches. In the sketchbook the accent falls on the work which lies between the original conception of the whole and the completed creation.

We return now to the sketchbook itself.

Amongst the drafts for the symphony there are, in addition to the variations on the English folksong already mentioned, the following pieces:

(p. 25) some passages from C. P. E. Bach's *Litanies* for double choir;[3]

(pp. 28 and 29) drafts for unknown marches;

(pp. 44–47, 57 and 58) drafts for the three marches for piano duet, Op. 45;

(p. 59) the first stages of an unknown piece for four string instruments;

(pp. 62 and 63) a draft for the song 'Das Glück der Freundschaft', Op. 88;

and (p. 64) a melody used later in the Pastoral Symphony:

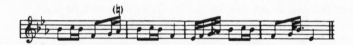

Evidently Beethoven did not allow much else to disturb his work on the *Sinfonia Eroica*.

The first sketches for the duet marches are rather far from the printed form. Whole sections of them and numerous passages are sketched again and again, and are quite different every time. The beginning of the first march in its original version is as follows:

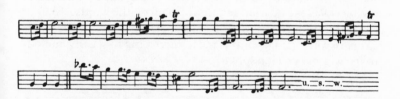

The position of these sketches shows that they were written while Beethoven was working on the Funeral March of the symphony. The unknown marches mentioned above, of which one (p. 28)

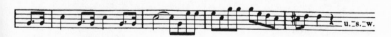

is taken up again later (on p. 93), appear to have been intended for the same collection.[4]

Beethoven writes down the entire text and vocal part of the song 'Das Glück der Freundschaft'. The vocal part is in the treble clef and it is only the German text that is added. Since there are no shorter sketches before it, and since the sketch is little changed and is, apart from a few trifling differences, the same as the printed version, we can be certain that this is not a true first draft; the song was already finished before and, as in the case of other songs, was written down here only for the purposes of publication.[5]

The sketches for the *Sinfonia Eroica* are followed immediately (apart from a few short sketches for unknown pieces) by some short keyboard exercises (p. 93), drafts for an unknown march cited above, and (p. 96) the following with its note:

Pages 96–120 contain sketches for two pieces from the Schikaneder opera which, before starting on *Leonore*, Beethoven was intending to write for the Theater an der Wien.[6] The first of the pieces is the quartet, left unfinished, on the words, 'Blick, o Herr, durch diese Bäume', from which a melody in the opera *Leonore* was later taken. It is most interesting to see this melody in its original version (p. 110):

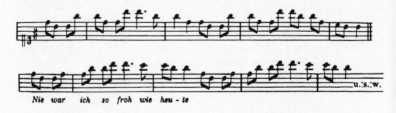

je grösser der Bach je tiefer der Ton: the greater the stream, the lower the note. [Transl.]

The second piece was intended to become an aria but it remained in sketches. The words

Hört, Rachegötter, mich	Hear me, O vengeful gods,
Und Rache schenket mir!	And vengeance grant me,
Als Sklave will ich ewig	And I, your slave, will be
Euch zinsbar sein dafür. u.s.w.	In your eternal debt. etc.

can only have been meant to be sung by the unnamed rival; we conclude that the aria follows the quartet above, and so the quartet cannot be a finale as has elsewhere been assumed.

Among the operatic sketches appear the following:

(p. 97) a few attractive melodies, which look like folk-tunes:

(p. 107) scale exercises etc.

(p. 116) the beginnings of an Adagio for piano, and sketches for a setting of words by Gellert, which have however nothing in common with the printed composition (Op. 48 no. 3):[7]

Denk, o Mensch, an dei - nen Tod. Säu - me nicht, denn Eins ist noth.

(p. 117) the first stages of a sonata for piano 'con Violoncello', and an unknown piano piece;

(p. 118) a 2-part canon, and the beginning of a piece for 'Viole, Vclli, Corno e Contrabasso';

(p. 119) the start of a polyphonic composition with the text 'Tibi gratulor';

(p. 120) the start of a piece with the curious title 'Quartetto per 4 voci zugleich gut für den letzten Zug vom Pianoforte' and several other unfinished sketches.

The fact that Beethoven could think of so much at once indicates that he was not constrained by his work on the opera but on the contrary was busy with new compositions.

The keyboard exercises already mentioned are similar to others we find elsewhere:

It is certain that they were not merely written down; Beethoven will also have played them, together with others which were not written out. It is reasonable to assume that the attention to keyboard technique and this particular type of exercise had some influence on the brilliant passage-work of a piano composition started shortly after these sketches were written.

The composition in question is the first movement of the Sonata in C major, Op. 53, the sketches for which (pp. 120–132) begin just after those on the opera. Beethoven plunges almost immediately into the main theme:

Herewith the predominant character of the piece is established. Gradually the other constituent sections appear in other short sketches, and longer ones combine the various fragments. As can be seen in the above sketch, the first two bars of the principal theme appear in the first stage of work only in semiquavers, and do not come also in quavers until later, during the work on the second part of the movement. The motive in the fourth bar of the theme is always without the acciaccatura, as above. The ornament was therefore probably added only in the fair copy. The melody of the first part of the second group (p. 123) originally lacked some of the beauty it later acquired:

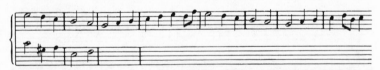

The fact that its key here is C major does not necessarily mean that it was intended to appear in this key; against such an assumption we should note that the sketch does not occur in context. Other passages, for instance (on p. 122) the transition to the second group

and on the same page a point towards the end of the exposition

had originally less flow than in the form we know. Of some interest is the first draft (p. 123) of a passage at the beginning of the recapitulation:

In order to give the first subject at its re-entry a different air and colouring, Beethoven inserts a digressive episode in a remote key. Here, as everywhere, the final version is preferable, achieving the same end more succinctly. The rather lengthy and sequential spinning-out of a subsidiary motive, as in the sketch, would have separated too far the first and second statements of the first subject to the detriment of the flow of the music. It is also to be seen that in the coda, shortly before the end of the movement, there was originally no ritardando (p. 131):

The ritardando of the printed version is due to a later modification. Once more the final version is preferable, since after the slowing-down the shortened first subject has a more striking effect.

The sketches for the sonata movement are interrupted by those for the Andante in F major for piano (pp. 121–137) and those for the last movement of the sonata Op. 53 (pp. 126–145). This supports and confirms what Ferdinand Ries tells us (*Biographische Notizen*, p. 101): the Andante in F originally belonged to the Op. 53 sonata.

The principal subject of the Andante arose partly from a process of combination; first an Andante in E major is started (p. 121):

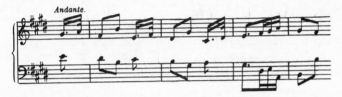

Immediately after this Beethoven begins again; the opening of the first sketch is somewhat changed and then continued:

Shortly before the end of this sketch, which breaks off like the previous one, there comes a phrase which is now established as the core of a new melody. Beethoven changes the key, brings the phrase to the beginning, and writes:

The first part of the principal subject is now almost complete, but not the second part. On p. 125 Beethoven returns to the motive with which the second part in the second sketch begins:

He retains the key of D-flat major from the third sketch and changes the melody which occurs in this key. The D-flat melody is now rejected and another voice secondary (or perhaps more accurately *primary*) to it takes its place. The beginning of the second section now receives a different treatment (p. 127):

This comes close to the final version, which is very nearly fixed in a sketch on p. 131:

From the remaining sketches we here select the first draft of the middle subject (p. 135), where the theme runs more smoothly than in the printed version:

and the first two drafts for the coda (pp. 133, 135):

These show that the reaching of G-flat major was decided right from the start, though not so the return to the principal subject in this key, which only happened in a subsequent sketch.

For the last movement of the Op. 53 sonata a different opening was intended originally (p. 125):

Beethoven rejected this opening, but retained one of its features, namely the first note and the pedal effect with it. Page 134

contains what is to be regarded as the first sketch for the last movement of the sonata in its present form:

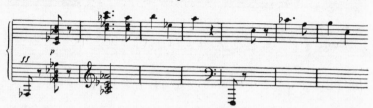

As with the first movement, Beethoven here plunges immediately *in medias res*, and thereby the heart of the principal subject, at least in its rhythm, is found. It can also be seen that the use of the pedal is an essential characteristic of the passage. The principal subject had to undergo some changes before it acquired its final form. The different versions can be seen in the following sketches:

(p. 138)

(p. 139)

(p. 139)

(There is in fact a sketch for the main theme several pages earlier, but this was written down later. It corresponds to the opening of one of the sketches above and can therefore be omitted here.)

A small but effective change brings us to the second of the middle subjects. One of the first sketches for it begins on p. 136 like this:

Another sketch near it on the same page corresponds rhyth-mically and is here omitted. In a sketch which follows soon after this (p. 141) the final note of the basic motive is resolved into two quavers:

Beethoven here evidently envisaged a caesura after the eighth (and not after the seventh) note. (A motive which is rhythmically similar is to be found in the final movement of the Op. 26 sonata.) Later Beethoven placed an anticipatory quaver before the first-appearing motive. The caesura is thereby shifted and the rhythm modified.

Other notable features are 1. that the figuration at the begin-ning of the first middle subject was originally conceived in a narrower compass (p. 137):

2. that this middle subject, as can be seen in the following sketch, originally lacked its end-piece (p. 139):

109

and 3. that the Rondo was originally intended to have a much briefer ending (p. 138):

The coda of the final, printed version, in which some of this *presto* survives, was also originally conceived in $^2/_4$ time; it can only have acquired its ₵ time through the appearance of the main theme in augmentation. But the final *prestissimo* which we know is considerably richer than this *presto*, which moves above the tonic and dominant alone.[8]

Among the last sketches for the Rondo we find on p. 145 the start of a setting of the Klopstock song 'Das Rosenband':

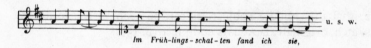

and (pp. 145–147) drafts of an Allegretto for piano (unpublished):[9]

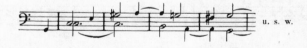

In the middle of the work on this Allegretto begin some drafts for Marcellina's aria from the opera *Leonore* (pp. 146–155) and soon after this for the next four numbers of the opera (pp. 148–171).

We can deduce from the position of these sketches that Marcellina's aria was begun when the Op. 53 sonata was finished in the sketches; but only a short time can have passed between the end of the work on the sonata and the beginning of that on the aria, since the Allegretto overlaps with both the Rondo and the aria. There is no doubt that we have here the first work on the opera *Leonore*.[10]

There are four major sketches for this aria and a fair number of smaller ones, which are partly contained also in the longer sketches. These longer sketches differ in most passages. The first of them (p. 147)

O wär ich schon mit dir ver-eint und dürf-te Mann dich nen-nen!

bears no resemblance to any of the arrangements known either in print or from transcripts, apart from a running passage in the interlude. But the second sketch (p. 150)

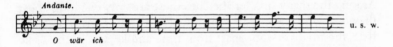

O wär ich

and the third, with its introduction of eight bars (p. 151)

and the fourth (p. 152)

O wär ich schon mit dir ver-

eint, und

show more similarity.

If we transfer the beginning of the second sketch to the last, we arrive at a piece which so closely resembles the arrangement in Otto Jahn's piano reduction of *Leonore* (pp. 178–182) that we have to regard this as the earliest of the printed arrangements.

Beethoven's method with the aria is to set about the whole

piece, but he works differently at the duet of Marcellina and Jaquino (pp. 148–171); here he takes at most only a few passages from the text and reworks them repeatedly, seeking to give the words a suitable melody and appropriate setting, e.g. (p. 157):

and (pp. 154 and 168):

Among the many smaller sketches there are only two long ones; they deal with the middle of the duet. The only correspondence with the final version, apart from time and key, is in the basic instrumental motive, which is in fact the essential core of the whole duet.

For the third piece from the opera there are several sketches of varying length (pp. 155–163), one of the last of them coming quite close to the final version:

In the fourth piece appropriate melodies are sought for the opening words (pp. 162 and 163); and the melodies appear quite different:

After this there are fragmentary sketches for some 4-part canons, in which some of the above themes are employed; we may conclude that the canonic treatment of this piece was decided from the start.

For the fifth piece there are four short sketches, all in F major, one of them as follows:

There is nowhere any correspondence with the printed version.

With the exception of Marcellina's aria none of these operatic pieces is completed in the sketches; work on the opera was left for the time being.

Among these pieces of work on the opera we find, in addition to a fair number of small sketches (omitted here), the following:

(p. 147) a passage for a letter;
(p. 148) the first four bars of the G major piano concerto:

(p. 151) sketches for some country dances;

(p. 155) the beginning of a *Fantasia un poco adagio* with the note '*si continua sempre molto semplice in questa maniera*' and a march-type piece, almost completed in draft;

(pp. 155 and 156) a draft for the third movement of the C minor symphony:

Notable features here include the opening without its upbeat and anticipatory bar, and the progress of a middle voice entering in bar 18 and returning in a different position eight bars later.

On pp. 157 f. there are sketches for the first movement of the same symphony:[11]

(p. 158) unused sketches of a composition for strings and brass, with the note '*könnte zuletzt endigen mit einem Marsch*' (could end with a march);

(p. 159) a theme with the start of a variation for piano, and a fragment of a piece entitled *lustige Sinfonia;* also on this page the theme for a fugue in a Kyrie;

(p. 165) a keyboard exercise;

(p. 166) a piece with an opening reminiscent of an aria in Haydn's *The Seasons*:

Also here the start of an Agnus Dei etc.

It is evident from this collection of sketches that Beethoven was still busy with many other compositions when he was working at the five operatic pieces; thus there cannot have been any urgency about the work on *Leonore*, and the time had yet to come when Beethoven was to turn his attention almost exclusively to the opera.

The passage of the letter mentioned above runs as follows: *Da übrigens ihr Brief in einem Ton geschrieben ist, der mir ganz fremd und ungewöhnlich ist, so kann ich nichts anderes thun, als ihren Brief zurücksenden, wovon ich zu meiner Rechtfertigung eine Abschrift habe machen lassen.* (Since your letter is written in a tone to which I am quite unaccustomed, I have no option but to return your letter; I have for my vindication had a copy made of it.) Beethoven must have received an unpleasant letter, which he wished to answer in this way. The circumstances of the letter and the intended recipient of this reply are uncertain, but there may be some connection with the argument Beethoven had in 1803 with Artaria or Mollo over the printing of the Quintet Op. 29.[12]

Straight after the work on *Leonore* follow sketches (pp. 172–179) for two passages in the oratorio *Christus am Ölberge* (*The Mount of Olives*); they are the second half of the first aria and the end of the second number (pp. 14–18 and 29–48 of the score in the collected edition). What we have here are however not the first sketches for these pieces, but reworkings. That they were intended as revisions is evident primarily because the sketches deal only with separate parts or sections of longer pieces, and the parts preceding the passages found in the sketchbook, and out of which these passages arise thematically, are not touched on. Secondly, in some of the longer sketches that appear, passages in which the vocal line is silent for several bars are filled out, not with the leading motives as in other sketches for vocal compositions, but with the instrumental bass part, or the accompanying violin part, or with rests. This is sure evidence that when Beethoven wrote these drafts he had the completed score before him. We cannot say anything certain about the relation of the sketches to the earlier version, since no other arrangement survives, apart from the printed one, and this is produced in the sketches. We must remain content with examining the sketches themselves; only on them can we base any conjectures.

Of the sketches for the first number most are directed at the closing section of the aria. The setting of the words '*Nimm den Leidenskelch von mir*' ('Take the cup of sorrow from me') differ very widely. The composer seeks a musical expression appropriate to their content, and this expression ranges from utter dejection to passionate pathos (p. 173):

(p. 173):

(p. 175):

(p. 179):

It seems from these different versions that the aim of all the reworking was an effective ending.

The sketches for the second number are mostly concerned with the solo part and begin at the point where in the final version the choir and soloist meet (p. 29, bar 3 in the score of the collected edition). The evidence of these sketches suggests that in the original version the solo part was silent from the entry of the chorus onwards, and that the object here was to extend it to the end of the movement.[13]

Among these sketches are (on p. 177) the first stages of three pieces: a 'Sinfonia in D minor', a piano piece, and a *Zapfenstreich* (tattoo). As Beethoven used for these pieces a page previously left blank, we should not assume that they constitute an interruption in the earlier work.

On pp. 180–182, in addition to some unknown pieces, there are drafts for the first movement of the Triple Concerto, Op. 56. Their character shows that this was the first stage of the work's composition. The original form of the first subject is as follows:

Later it becomes:

Work on this concerto was continued in a later sketchbook.

This brings us to the end of the sketchbook; there remains only a note on the inside back cover: '*Sonata scritta in un stilo [brillante]* molto concertante quasi come d'un Concerto*'. This is the title of the Op. 47 sonata. Perhaps Beethoven wrote it down while he was occupied with the fair copy of one of the pieces appearing in the sketchbook.[14]

At the beginning of this essay we took October 1802 and April 1804 as the furthest termini between which the sketchbook can belong. Naturally we assume that the compositions worked on in the book originated during this period in the order in which they appear. If we disregard less important details and consider that the smaller compositions must have been completed before the longer ones among which they appear, we may establish the following chronological order for the finished or partially finished works:

Variations on 'Rule Britannia',
1st movement of the 3rd symphony,
3 marches for piano duet,

*crossed out

The song 'Das Glück der Freundschaft' Op. 88,

2nd, 3rd and 4th movements of the 3rd symphony,

Quartet for the Schikaneder opera (unfinished),

1st movement of the sonata Op. 53,

Andante in F major for piano,

Last movement of the sonata Op. 53,

Bagatelle in C major (not printed),

The first 5 vocal numbers of the opera *Leonore* (preliminary work),

1st movement of the Piano Concerto in G major (only the opening bars),

1st and 3rd movements of the Symphony in C minor (only separate passages, preliminary work),

Two passages from the oratorio *The Mount of Olives* (revision)

1st movement of the Triple Concerto Op. 56 (preliminary work).

NOTES

1. The variations on 'Rule Britannia' appeared on June 20th 1804. The theme, reputedly composed by Dr T. A. Arne in 1740, is found written out in Beethoven's hand amongst sketches for the second and fourth movements of the second symphony. So Beethoven must have become acquainted with it not later than 1802.

2. The revised copy of the full score of the third symphony kept in the archives of the Gesellschaft der Musikfreunde in Vienna has the following title, including some words which are erased:

Sinfonia grande
intitulata Bonaparte
1804 im August
del Sigr.
Louis van Beethoven.
geschrieben
auf Bonaparte

Sinfonie 3.   *Op. 55.*

(The original title, written in ink in the hand of the copyist, comprised only the 1st, 2nd, 4th and 5th lines. The 2nd line was later erased and lines 6 and 7 were added by Beethoven himself in pencil. Another unknown hand later inserted line 3 and another again still later added line 8.) The date given (August 1804) cannot be taken as the date of completion of the work; in the light of other statements it is untenable. Ferdinand Ries (*Biographische Notizen*, p. 77) recounts that Beethoven had intended to dedicate the symphony to Bonaparte when he was First Consul, but when he learned that Bonaparte had declared himself Emperor he tore up the title page of a copy of the symphony and it was then that the original title 'Bonaparte' was changed. If the story is true—and it is certainly credible—then the copy concerned, and hence the symphony itself, must have been finished by May 1804 at the latest, for Bonaparte became Emperor on May 18th. Ries says further (*op. cit.* p. 77) that the symphony was composed at Heiligenstadt in 1802. Carl Czerny gives 1803 as the year of the composition. Beethoven's countryman J. Mähler said that he had found him occupied in finishing the symphony in the autumn of 1803 and heard him play the Finale. (cf.

Thayer's biography, vol. II pp. 236 and 392).* According to these statements the symphony must have been completed or nearly completed by the end of 1803 at the latest. Ries may still be right if by 'composed' we understand 'begun'.

3.   This work was published in Copenhagen in 1786 under the title 'Zwey Litaneyen aus dem Schleswig-Holsteinischen Gesangbuche mit ihrer bekannten Melodie für Acht Singstimmen in zwei Chören . . . gesetzt von Carl Ph. E. Bach'. The composer describes it in a letter as one of his most powerfully written pieces. Beethoven appears to have had a high opinion of the *Litanies*. An entry in his diary of 1818 shows a yearning for the work while he was preparing the second Mass: 'Bach's Litanies not to be forgotten'.

4.   The Op. 45 marches appeared on March 10th 1804. According to a note by Czerny they were composed in the Eckhaus am Peter in Vienna, now Peters-Platz No. 14, where Beethoven lived during the period roughly from the beginning of November 1802 to not later than April 1803.

5.   The earliest edition of the song bears the title 'Das Glück der Freundschaft. in Music gesetzt van Bethoven. bey Löschenkohl in Wien. 1803'. I was unable to discover the month and day of publication. In March 1804 the song was reprinted; according to this the publication of the first edition should be placed in the second half of 1803.

6.   In a letter written in Vienna at the end of February 1813 and printed in the *Leipziger allgemeine musikalische Zeitung* on March 30th of that year we read: 'Beethoven and Abt Vogler are each composing an opera for the Theater an der Wien.' *Der Freimüthige*, April 12th 1803 reports: 'Beethoven was recently engaged for a handsome salary at the Theater an der Wien', and on May 17th: 'He [Beethoven] will write one opera and Abt Vogler three. In payment, apart from accommodation, they receive 10 per cent of the takings for the first ten performances.' An announcement in a report in the *Zeitung für die elegante Welt*, August 2nd, written on June 19th in Vienna, reads: 'The Abbé Vogler is now writing an opera to a libretto by H. [Huber], and Beethoven one to a libretto by Schikaneder.' There is no doubt that the opera referred to in these reports is the one to which the sketches belong. One more intimation is by Beethoven himself, who writes to his friend Macco on November 3rd 1803: 'But it is impossible for me at the moment to write this oratorio immediately, because I am now just *starting work on my opera*'.** How-

---

*The references to Thayer are of course to the first (German) edition. In the new English edition, revised and edited by Elliot Forbes, pp. 324–362 should be referred to *passim*. [Transl.]

**This letter is to be found in Emily Anderson's translation, Vol I pp. 99–100. In *Beethoveniana* pp. 82–99 Nottebohm has an article containing more information about the opera, including what survives of the text. [Transl.]

ever the opera meant here is probably *Leonore*. On the evidence of these passages it is probable that the sketches in the book were written between February and July 1803, though possibly not until October or November of that year.

7.   The songs of Gellert Op. 48 are said to have been composed in 1803, and were published between the end of 1803 and March 1804.

8.   The sonata Op. 53 appeared in May 1805 and the Andante in F major in May 1806. According to Otto Jahn the pieces were composed in 1804. He does not say on what evidence this statement is based.

9.   Beethoven later inscribed on the work: 'Bagatelle No. 5'.

10.   The position of the 'Leonore' pieces in the sketchbook suggests that they came not more than about three months after the abandoned pieces for the Schikaneder opera. Judging by the dates given above (see note 6) the composition of *Leonore* was probably begun between May and October 1803, or possibly not until January or February 1804. The second terminus ante quem is to be considered the latest possible. Statements in the biographies are irreconcilable with this deduction; so for instance in Thayer's biography (Vol. II pp. 263 and 267) we read that Beethoven was commissioned at the end of 1804 to write an opera for the Theater an der Wien and received the text for *Fidelio* (*Leonore*) in the winter of 1804–1805. The same assertion is found in Schindler's biography, Vol. I p. 118).* The source for both of these is in fact an article by Friedrich Treitschke in *Orpheus für das Jahr 1841* (p. 258).**

The biographers have, quite naturally, accepted what Treitschke said, since there was no evidence to the contrary. But the evidence of the sketchbook demands that we examine the source for these statements more closely.

Treitschke has given no proof for the correctness of his statement; furthermore his claim is not supported or confirmed by any other observation or report dating from before 1805. At the time Treitschke either did not know Beethoven at all or did not know him well enough to be sufficiently well informed about his activities and intentions. This is revealed by his own words; he occasionally says of the revision of *Leonore* undertaken in 1804 that he had 'recently become a close friend of Beethoven'. There is no indication—indeed it is improbable—that at the time in question, in 1803 and 1804, Treitschke was so well acquaint-

---

*In the modern English edition (*Beethoven as I knew him*) see p. 122. [Transl.]

**Treitschke writes: 'It was at the end of 1804 when Freiherr von Braun, the new owner of the royal private Theater an der Wien, employed L. v. B., who was now a young man at the peak of his abilities, to write an opera for this theatre. In addition to an honorarium he was offered free accommodation in the theatre building. Joseph Sonnleithner undertook to provide the text, and chose the French book *l'Amour Conjugal*, though it had already been set to music by Gaveaux and also in Italian by Paer (as *Leonore*); both these arrangements had been translated into German. Beethoven did not fear his predecessors and devoted himself utterly to the work, which by the middle of 1805 was nearly complete.'

ed with the circumstances and occurrences in the Theater an der Wien that his statements can be considered reliable; it must be remembered that Treitschke was in any case engaged at another theatre and was therefore not in close touch with the undertakings of the Theater an der Wien.* His testimony for the time of the third arrangement of *Leonore* can be defended, but not for that of the first arrangement. More accurate witnesses are probably to be found in Ferdinand Ries, the only pupil Beethoven had at that time, and J. v. Seyfried, who was then conductor at the theatre for which Beethoven's opera was written; the information these two men give agrees with what we gather from the sketchbook, but not with Treitschke's assertion. Ries tells us (op. cit. p. 112), 'when he (Beethoven) was composing *Leonore* he had free accommodation for a year at the Wiedner [*sic*] Theater,** but since this was not near enough to the courtyard he was not happy with it and rented lodgings in the red house at the Alserkaserne'. Beethoven lived in the theatre building from May 1803 and in the red house in the spring of 1804. Seyfried states (*Studien*, App. p. 8), 'Sonnleithner took on the task of adapting the Singspiel *Leonore* for the operatic society of the Theater an der Wien; Beethoven there received free accommodation and set to work with heart and soul'. According to this account the composition was begun soon after Beethoven's move into the theatre, that is at any rate some time in 1803.

Our assumption that Beethoven started composing *Leonore* at the latest in February 1804 is compatible with other evidence which needs a great deal of explaining when combined with what has been hitherto assumed. First of all it is inconceivable that Beethoven composed the opera in the short period between the winter of 1804–1805 and around October 1805.*** It is clear from the nature of this work and the evidence of other compositions (which provide a yardstick) that Beethoven must have spent more than a full year on it. Secondly our assumption explains the serious rivalry with Ferdinand Paer. The *Leipziger allgemeine musikalische Zeitung* reported on October 24th 1804 that Paer's new opera *Leonore* was being well received in Dresden. (The first Dresden performance took place on October 3rd 1804). If we are to believe Treitschke, the theatre management shortly afterwards chose the same subject for Beethoven, without considering that Paer's opera would soon find its way also to Vienna (as had almost all the other operas of this then so popular composer) and that as it became known it

---

*Friedrich Treitschke, b. 1776 in Leipzig, came to the Hofschauspieltheater in Vienna as an actor in 1800. In 1802 he became producer and librettist at the Hofoper and kept this position until 1809, when he went to the Theater an der Wien.

**Occasionally spelt this way in jest. [Transl.]

***We have to bear in mind here the date of the first performance (20th November 1805), the necessary rehearsals, the copying of parts, etc.

would prejudice the chances of success of another opera with the same name and content.* But the matter is very simple if we look at the evidence of the sketchbook. Beethoven's work was begun earlier, and by the time Paer's opera became known the work was far enough advanced for its abandonment to be unthinkable. Thirdly our assumption offers an explanation for why Sonnleithner, for his rendering of the libretto, used only the French text and did not consider Paer's in many ways preferable Italian text; he had to do this, because the latter text did not yet exist. Fourthly, the subsequent change of title from *Leonore* to *Fidelio* and Beethoven's refusal to accept the new title appear in a different light. We can well understand why the management of the theatre insisted on changing the original title after Paer's *Leonore* became known; it was a necessity for the theatre. If however, as Treitschke claims, the libretto was written only after Paer's opera became known, why was this course not followed from the beginning, and a name given to Beethoven's opera which differed from that of Paer's? The fact is that Beethoven was later unwilling to appear apprehensive of a rivalry with Paer by accepting the changed title (*Fidelio*).

Certain other of Treitschke's statements are similarly dubious. His claim that Beethoven was offered his free accommodation in the theatre at the end of 1804 is probably based on a confusion with the events of 1803. There are letters to verify that Beethoven was living there in May and June 1803, but no such evidence for the end of 1804 or later. Also doubtful in Treitschke's account is the statement that Beethoven took no part in the choice of libretto. It is just as likely that Beethoven had some say in this as it is that his reason for abandoning the Schikaneder opera was simply his refusal to set such a text.

We shall not dwell on Treitschke's statements or on the conclusions that have been drawn from them. It is for further research to narrow down the space of time (May 1803 to February 1804) in which we have established the inception of the work on *Leonore*.

11.   Sketches for the G major piano concerto and the C minor symphony are found together also on other pages. Cf. my *Beethoveniana*, p. 10 f., though the evidence of the present sketchbook necessitates some changes on p. 16. I did not have this evidence at the time of writing.

12.   Cf. *Beethoveniana* p. 3. If we surmised correctly on p. 116 above, the passage of the letter must have been written soon after January 22nd 1803.

13.   *Christus am Ölberge* (*The Mount of Olives*) was first performed on

*The three years 1799–1801 saw the performances of seven new operas by Paer in the Wiener Hoftheater. *Achille* was performed fifty-five times in the three years 1801–1803, *Poche ma Buone* fourteen times in 1801, and so on. Paer's *Leonore* received its first Vienna performance in 1805 and five subsequent performances in the same year.

April 5th 1803. Subsequent performances took place on August 4th 1803, March 27th 1804 etc. It is unlikely that the revision of these passages was made very long after the first performance. Other sketches show that Beethoven worked extensively on the oratorio in 1802.

14. The Op. 47 sonata was submitted for publication to Simrock on May 25th 1803 and the contract was signed on February 3rd 1804. The dedication to R. Kreutzer followed not later than September 1804. Since this dedication is lacking in the note on the cover of the book, the note must have been written not later than this date.

INDEX OF NAMES

Adamer, J., 39
Anderson, Emily, 5, 40n., 121n.
André, Johann (publisher), 43
Arne, Dr T. A., 120
Artaria and Co. (publishers), 40, 116
Bach, Carl Philipp Emmanuel, 99, 121
Bonaparte, Napoleon, 120
Braun, Baron Peter von, 122n.
Cappi, Giovanni, (publisher), 43
Clary, Countess Josephine von, see Klary, Countess Josepha von.
Czerny, Carl, 42, 43, 120, 121
Duport, Louis Antoin, 40 f.
Eybler, Joseph, 39
Friederich, Johann Baptist, 40
Fuchs, Johann, 39
Gaveaux, Pierre, 122n.
Gellert, C. F. (poet), 101, 122
Gesellschaft der Musikfreunde, 120
Haslinger, Tobias, (publisher), 40 f.
Haydn, Franz Joseph, 39
Heiligenstadt, 40, 42, 43, 120
Henneberg, Johann Baptist, 39
Hetzendorf, 43
Höllmayr, A., 39
Hörmann, J., 39
Jahn, Otto, 111, 122
Kerman, Joseph, x, xi
Kessler, J. C., 3
Klary, Countess Josepha von, 41

Klopstock, Friedrich Gottlieb (poet), 110
Kreutzer, Rodolphe, 125
Leipziger allgemeine musikalische Zeitung, 21, 41, 42, 121, 123
Lipavsky, Joseph, 39
Löschenkohl (publisher), 121
Macco, Alexander, 121
Mähler, Willibrord Joseph, 120
Mandyczewski, Eusebius, x
Marx, Adolph Bernard, 97
Matthisson, Friedrich von (poet), 9, 37
Metastasio, Pietro (poet), 11
Mollo and Co. (publishers), 39, 116
Mozart, Wolfgang Amadeus, 39
Naegeli, Hans Georg, 43
Oberdöbling, 43
Paer, Ferdinand, 122n., 123 f.
Pichl, Wenzeslaus, 39
Ries, Ferdinand, 42, 43, 105, 120 f., 123.
von Rossi, 39
Schikaneder, Emanuel, 100, 119, 121, 122 ff.
Schindler, Anton, viii, 4, 40, 41, 43, 122
Schmidt, Dr Johann Adam, 40
Seyfried, Ignaz von, 39, 123
Simrock and Co. (publishers), 43
Sonnleithner, Joseph Ferdinand, 122n., 123 f.
Stein, Carl, 3

Steiner, S. A. and Co. (publishers), 40

Süssmayr, Franz Xaver, 39

Teyber, Anton, 39

Teyber, Franz, 39

Thayer, Alexander Wheelock, vii, 43n., 121, 122

Theater an der Wien, 40, 100, 121, 122 f.

Treitschke, Georg Friedrich, 122 ff.

Vogler, Abbé Georg Joseph, 121

Wegeler, Franz Gerhard, 4, 5, 39, 40

Wiener Zeitung, 39, 40

Zeitung für die elegante Welt, 121

INDEX OF COMPOSITIONS

Op. 28, Piano sonata in D major, 42

Op. 29, Quintet in C major for two violins, two violas and 'cello, 116

Op. 30 no. 1, Sonata in A major for piano and violin, 19 f., 26, 27, 31, 37, 42

Op. 30 no. 2, Sonata in C minor for piano and violin, 22 f., 24, 25 f., 37

Op. 30 no. 3, Sonata in G major for piano and violin, 26, 29, 31, 32, 37

Op. 31 no. 1, Piano sonata in G major, 33 ff., 36, 37, 38

Op. 31 no. 2, Piano sonata in D minor, 26, 27 f., 37, 43

Op. 33 no. 6, Bagatelle in D major for piano, 12, 37, 40

Op. 34, Six variations in F major for piano, 32, 38, 43

Op. 35, Variations in E-flat for piano (*Eroica*), 32, 38, 42 f.

Op. 36, Symphony no. 2 in D major, 11, 13 ff., 37, 40

Op. 43, Ballet music for *Die Geschöpfe des Prometheus*, 42 f.

Op. 45, Three marches for piano duet, 99, 121

Op. 47, Sonata in A major for piano and violin, 20, 22, 32, 37, 42, 118, 125

Op. 53, Piano sonata in C major, 103 f., 105, 107 ff., 122

Op. 55, Symphony no. 3 in E-flat 1st movt., 50 ff., 120 f.

                                   2nd movt., 50, 81 ff.

                                     3rd movt., 88 ff.

                                     4th movt., 50, 94 ff.

Op. 56, Concerto in C major for piano, violin and 'cello, 118

Op. 58, Piano concerto no. 4 in G major, 69, 124

Op. 65, Scena and aria for Soprano, *Ah perfido*, 41

Op. 67, Symphony no. 5 in C minor, 114 f., 124

Op. 68, Symphony no. 6 in F major, the 'Pastoral' 99 f.

Op. 72 a. *Leonore*

         Aria (Marcellina), 111

         Duet (Marcellina and Jaquino), 112

         Terzet (Marcellina, Jaquino and Rocco), 112

         Quartet (Marcellina, Leonore, Jaquino and Rocco) 112 f.

         Aria (Rocco), 113

Op. 72 b. *Fidelio, see* Op. 72 a. and sketches for the Schikaneder opera.

Op. 85, *The Mount of Olives*, 116, 124 f.

Op. 88, *Das Glück der Freundschaft*, song for solo voice and piano, 100, 121

Op. 111, Piano sonata in C minor, 41
Op. 116, Terzet, *Tremate, empi, tremate,* for soprano, tenor, bass and orchestra, 19, 37, 40 f.
Op. 119 no. 5, Bagatelle in C minor, 26, 37
Op. 121 b., Matthisson's *Opferlied* for solo soprano, choir and orchestra, 9 f., 37

Piano works

Five variations in D on *Rule Britannia*, 50, 99, 120
Andante in F, 105 f.
Keyboard exercises, 100 f., 115
Marches (sketches), 99 f.
Other sketches, 26, 35 f., 101, 110, 114, 118, 122

Instrumental works

Country dances, 12, 37, 40, 114
Ländler, 19, 37, 39, 40
Minuets, 9, 39
Other sketches, 12, 19, 26, 32 f., 35, 99, 101, 115
Tattoo, 118

Vocal works

Sketches for the Schikaneder opera, 100 f., 121
Matthisson's *Opferlied, see* Op. 121 b.
Vom Tode by Gellert, 101, 122
Das Rosenband by Klopstock, 110
Zur Erde sank die Ruh' vom Himmel nieder, 50
Recitative and aria *No, non turbarti* by Metastasio, 10, 37
Kyrie and Agnus Dei, 115

Transcriptions

Canon on *Ein anders ist's das erste Jahr*, 20
C. P. E. Bach, from *zweichörige Litaneien*, 99, 121